Let It Shine

ANDREA DAVIS PINKNEY

Let It Shine

Stories of Black Women Freedom Fighters

Illustrated by

STEPHEN ALCORN

sandpiper

HOUGHTON MIFFLIN HARCOURT

Boston   New York

It is with tremendous gratitude that I thank Paula J. Reedy,
whose research assistance helped make this book possible.
—A.D.P.

The display type was set in Celestia Italic.
The text type was set in Cloister Old Style.
The illustrations are oil on canvas.

The Library of Congress has cataloged the hardcover edition as follows:
Pinkney, Andrea Davis.
Let it shine: stories of Black women freedom fighters / Andrea Davis Pinkney; illustrated by Stephen Alcorn.
p. cm.
"Gulliver Books."
Includes biographical references.
[1. Afro-American women—Civil rights workers—Biography. 2. Afro-American—Civil rights—History.
3. United States—Race relations.] I. Alcorn, Stephen, ill. II. Title.
E185.96.P5   2000
323'.092'396073—dc21
[B] 99-42806

ISBN: 978-0-15-201005-8 hardcover
ISBN: 978-0-547-90604-1 paperback

Manufactured in China
SCP 10 9 8 7 6 5 4 3 2 1

4500383439

To Mom and Dad
—A. D. P.

To my mother and father,
who, by example shown, taught me the difference
between right and wrong
—S. A.

Contents

This Little Light of Mine

ON AUGUST 28, 1963, one month before I was born, my father stood on Washington D.C.'s great lawn and listened with rapt attention to Dr. Martin Luther King Jr. delivering his unforgettable "I Have a Dream" speech. Just blocks away, in my parents' tiny apartment in southeast Washington, my pregnant mother watched the history-making event on television. Mom says I kicked and squirmed inside her belly throughout Dr. King's powerful speech. And though I was yet to be born, the March on Washington became my earliest experience with the civil rights movement. But there would be countless others.

My father began his career as one of the first black congressional interns on Capitol Hill. His personal mission was to learn the inner workings of Congress so that he could one day use his knowledge to move the civil rights cause forward. Dad would later do just that. For many years he worked for the U.S. Department of Labor, where he helped draft federal regulations implementing Executive Orders for affirmative action. He was a key player in making sure equal employment opportunities and ethical workplace standards were available to every wage earner in the United States.

My mother, an active member of both the National Coalition of One Hundred

Black Women, a black women's advocacy group, and Delta Sigma Theta Sorority, Inc., one of the largest African American civic service organizations in the United States, worked in an unofficial capacity alongside my father, where she, too, devoted herself to advancing the struggle.

Both my parents were—and still are—loyal supporters of the National Association for the Advancement of Colored People (NAACP), and throughout my childhood were committed to the grassroots efforts that comprised the civil rights movement. I spent many of my summer vacations at the annual conference for the National Urban League, one of America's leading black civil rights organizations, where, with my parents, I would listen to the speeches of an array of national civil rights leaders, such as John Jacob, former National Urban League president, and Dorothy Height, who was then the president of the National Council of Negro Women. These men and women urged us to work toward a vision of racial harmony in our communities. Memories of those summers, when I was steeped in the heart of social change, still live with me.

I also remember the early 1970s, when the civil rights movement took an upward swing. There were many times when I answered our kitchen telephone to hear the voice of civil rights leader Jesse Jackson or Benjamin Hooks, former president of the NAACP, asking to speak with my father. Dad would usually retreat to a quiet room when the calls came in so that he could speak in private.

I later learned that Jesse Jackson was calling to plot strategy and to gain my father's support for his Operation Bread Basket, a reform program that provided food and social services to Chicago's underprivileged African American community. Benjamin Hooks sought Dad's advice on NAACP program initiatives to promote fair housing and employment.

"Black empowerment" was more than a slogan in our home. It was a deeply held belief that my parents, through their example, instilled in their three children. To brand myself a product of the civil rights movement is no overstatement. So when in her brilliance, my editor Liz Van Doren approached me to write a collection of stories about black women freedom fighters, I said yes immediately. I *had* to write this book.

But then came a million questions. *What direction would the collection take? Which women would we include? How would the stories be told?*

After many long discussions with Liz, hours of reading and researching, and, of course, talks with Mom and Dad, I decided to focus the collection on ten women whose individual lives wove together one incredible story—a story of the challenges and triumphs of civil rights that spanned American history from the eighteenth century to the present day.

Goodness knows there are hundreds of women who, through their bravery, have changed the face of America. Since *all* of their stories cannot be told in a single book, I chose the women whose stories I found most compelling.

During the creation of this book, Liz and I endearingly called the ten women "our freedom fighters." We understood that as it pertains to the pursuit of racial justice, *freedom* means so much more than freedom from slavery. These women fought for many freedoms—freedom from sexism, oppression, the fear of being silenced. Freedom to choose housing, ride public transportation, and express themselves both in newspapers and on television.

Some of these women you may already know. Others you may be meeting for the very first time. A goal we worked toward when pulling this collection together was to put a new spin on some of the tried-and-true *she*roes of human equality, and to introduce some of those who have had just as strong an impact on social justice but whose praises have not been sung loudly enough.

Not every woman featured here lived to see the fruits of her labor. And though each freedom fighter worked tirelessly, some could not point to immediate results that stemmed from their actions. The real accomplishment of these amazing women is that they *spoke out* fearlessly. No matter what, these freedom fighters let their lights shine on the darkness of inequality.

It is my hope that the stories of the women presented here offer a window into their tremendous power. And I hope their lives reflect something in each of us—the courage to fight for what we believe is right, the willingness to stand up under fire and disadvantage, the serenity to carry on when self-doubt, weariness, and the ignorance of others stand in the way of progress, and the fortitude to keep one's eyes on those prizes that will lead to a better world.

—ANDREA DAVIS PINKNEY

Sojourner Truth

Born: Hurley, New York • 1797 (exact date unknown)
Died: Battle Creek, Michigan • November 26, 1883

"Ain't I a Woman?"

WHEN THE GOOD LORD was handing out the gift of conviction, he gave a hefty dose to Sojourner Truth. Born into slavery, she was given the slave-name Isabella. But most folks called her Belle. Belle's skin was as black as the blackest ebony wood, rich and dark and beautiful. And, oh, was she ever tall—a stately six feet by the time she was thirteen years old.

Belle and her parents lived on Charles Hardenbergh's tobacco farm, a piece of property nestled along the Hudson River in Hurley, New York.

Belle's mother, Mau-Mau Bett, had a special kind of strength. She was quiet strong, like a wind that keeps a boat on course. Belle's father, Baumfree, was backbone strong, like a tree that stands steady in a storm. Mau-Mau Bett and Baumfree needed every ounce of strength they could muster, to endure long hours of hard work plowing and harvesting their master's crops.

1

Belle was blessed with the strength of both her mother and her father—the quiet and the backbone. Mau-Mau Bett and Baumfree taught Belle to look hard times clear on in the eye, to wear her dignity like a well-stitched quilt, and to trust that God Almighty would bless her steps and always lead her right.

When Belle was eleven years old, she was sold away from her parents. She had no choice. In slavery times, somebody could buy you right up and take you away from all the people you loved. On the day she was first sold off, in 1808, the auctioneer man called out for an asking price. He asked who would pay top dollar for Belle. He told the people at the auction that she was as strong as a horse. That she had long fingers for picking lots of corn, and big feet for stomping beetles. Belle wanted to cry. Instead, she stood straight and steady on the auctioneer's block, praying and wondering.

Belle was purchased by a man named John Nealy, who owned a shop in Kingston, New York. But even then she knew she was more than a piece of merchandise. Someday, she vowed, she would fight to put an end to slavery's ugly way.

Separated from her mother and father, Belle soon learned that to endure she'd have to keep her head high and hold fast to the courage Mau-Mau Bett and Baumfree had taught her. Belle was sold to a new master in 1809, and to another a year later. Both of these masters owned land in New York State, and each was more vicious than the last. Belle worked long, hard days, busting firewood, shucking corn, hauling water, boiling potatoes—anything the master man wanted.

Finally one day Belle decided she'd had enough. On a twilit morning in 1826, she ran away, in search of freedom. She remembered what Mau-

Mau Bett and Baumfree had taught her about God leading her down the right path. And sure enough, the Almighty showed her the way.

Though Belle did not know where she was headed, her intuition led her to the cabin of a farmer she knew. The farmer had fallen ill and could not offer Belle a place to stay. But he showed her how to find the home of a Quaker couple, Isaac and Maria Van Wagener. He told her they were kindhearted people, abolitionists who hated the institution of slavery.

When Belle's current master, John Dumont, tracked her down at the Van Wagener farm, Isaac Van Wagener offered to buy Belle from him. Greediness got the best of John Dumont. He took Isaac's money and left Belle behind. Right then and there, Isaac freed Belle! And from that moment on, Belle was no longer enslaved.

Mau-Mau Bett and Baumfree had been right. Belle *was* blessed, indeed. In the years that followed, Belle traveled to New York City and worked as a maid—a *paid* maid. Now Belle was free to keep the vow she'd made to herself on the auction block: to help black folks find equality. But what, she wondered, could she—one black woman—do to help turn back the iron wheel of slavery?

Belle couldn't read or write, but she often asked others to read the Bible to her. She soon came to learn the Bible's words and could recite them, scripture and verse. For years Belle pondered the Good Book's wisdom. And all the while she prayed for guidance on how she could work to end slavery. At first no guidance came. Then on a summer morning in 1843, Inspiration whispered to Belle: *"Get yourself a new name, child. Live up to that name by preaching what's real and what's right."*

Belle settled on the name Sojourner Truth—a traveler who's telling it like it is. She thanked heaven's Lord for giving her a strong, memorable a copy of her book. Word of Sojourner spread, and soon people began to know her by name. She had become one of this country's most outspoken activists.

In 1852 Sojourner attended a women's rights convention in Akron, Ohio. Mercy, that place was a worm can of debate. People took turns speaking their minds, and each had a strong opinion. Many were well-respected clergymen who believed that men were entitled to superior rights and privileges because they were smarter than women. One minister said women didn't deserve the same as men because women were just plain weak. After all, he argued, men often helped women into carriages and carried them over ditches. Another minister claimed a woman's place was at home taking care of her children. And still another preacher declared that women must be inferior because God made Jesus a man.

Well, that was all the prompting Sojourner needed to get up and speak. She was the only black woman in the place, and when she stepped to the pulpit, some folks looked at her like she was a stain on their purest linens.

Sojourner started off slow and deliberate, using Mau-Mau Bett's quiet strength to speak. "You say women need to be helped into carriages and lifted over ditches. Nobody's *ever* helped me into a carriage or over a mud puddle. And ain't *I* a woman?"

Sojourner's voice rose to a fiery boom of truth—*her* truth. "Look at me!" she said, pulling back the sleeve on her solid, dark arm. "I have plowed, and I have planted. I have gathered into barns. No man could head me. And ain't *I* a woman?"

Sojourner kept on. Her mighty words set the room still. "You say Jesus was a man, so that means God favors men over women. Where did your Christ come from?" she asked. Then she summoned her father's backbone strength and stood tall to answer her own question. "Jesus came from God and a woman. Man had nothing to do with him."

Next Sojourner challenged the minister who had said women weren't as smart as men. "Suppose a man's mind holds a quart and a woman's don't hold but a pint; if her pint is full, it's as good as a quart."

When Sojourner stepped down from the pulpit, she was satisfied and proud. Indeed, speaking up and out was her God-given gift. A gift that sowed the seeds of freedom and equality.

Biddy Mason

Born: Hancock County, Mississippi • August 15, 1818
Died: Los Angeles, California • January 15, 1891

"If you hold your hand closed, nothing good can come in.
The open hand is blessed, for it gives in abundance, even as it receives."

THERE AREN'T MANY BOOKS written about Biddy Mason. But her achievements speak volumes about the drive and determination of women. If Biddy were alive today, we'd call her a mover and shaker. A history maker. One high-powered lady.

Biddy was born into slavery, with a rich mix of blood running through her veins. She was black and Native American. And her Native American ancestors came from three different Indian tribes: Choctaw, Seminole, and Geegi.

As a slave child, Biddy was bought and sold several times. She was moved from one plantation to another and had more masters than most slave children: Master Banks of Georgia, Master Crosby of Mississippi, and finally, Master John Smithson of South Carolina.

Biddy settled with the Smithson family, with whom she spent most of her childhood. As a slave she was forbidden to read. So Biddy gathered her smarts by *doing.*

And, oh, did Biddy *do.* At the Smithson house, it was Biddy's job to work alongside the house servants and the midwives. She baked bread, swept floors, polished silver, and helped birth babies.

Biddy became skilled at many types of household work, but in the eyes of John Smithson she was little more than a piece of property, like a teakettle or an embroidery sampler. In 1836, when Biddy was eighteen and had blossomed into a full-grown woman, John Smithson gave her and her two friends Hannah and Ella away as wedding gifts to his cousin Rebecca and Robert Marion Smith, Rebecca's new husband. That's when Biddy promised herself she would someday do something to stop the injustices of slavery.

Biddy, Hannah, and Ella served as Rebecca's house slaves. But it was Biddy's job to care for Rebecca, who became sickly shortly after she and Robert married. Soon Biddy had her own family to take care of as well. Robert Smith was the father of her three daughters: Ellen, born in 1838; Ann, born in 1844; and Harriet, born four years later.

Sometime around Ann's birth, Robert Smith became a member of the Church of Jesus Christ of Latter-Day Saints, the Mormons. He decided to move his family to Utah, where a large group of Mormons had settled.

In 1848 Robert Smith packed everything he owned—slaves, children, cattle, bedsheets, and frying pans—and set out on a long, slow journey to the West. The caravan included fifty-eight white people, thirty-four slaves, two yoke of oxen, seven milking cows, a slew of mules, and a whole lot of horses.

The trail was a hot, dusty rope that snaked its way through the prairie. On the trail, Biddy did what she knew best. She tended to folks by cooking, caring for children (her own and other people's), and delivering babies whenever an expectant mother said the time had come. Biddy seldom had the privilege of riding on one of the wagons. She *walked*—at the end of the line, where the trail grit was thickest.

Robert Smith stayed in Utah for three years. Then, in 1851, Brigham Young, the Mormon prophet, called for volunteers to establish a Mormon settlement in Southern California. So Smith set his wagon train on the trail to San Bernardino, California, seeking a new life in the state folks called gold country.

The trip to California was another arduous trek that allowed Biddy little time to rest. Since she'd left the South, Biddy had walked nearly two thousand miles! But on this journey, Biddy Mason had a plan that kept her weary feet going.

Biddy had learned that California was a free state, where slavery did not exist. Once she set foot on gold-country soil, she and her children could be as free as the wildflowers that covered the land. Biddy planned to live in California as a free woman. She didn't speak about her plan, of course. Biddy made the trip to California obediently, never once letting on that she had her sights set on freedom.

When Biddy arrived in California, it was golden indeed. She encountered all kinds of free black people—men and women who were bankers, nurses, barbers, state legislators, mail carriers, ranch hands, and even cowboys. She met members of the black community in Los Angeles, and some of them became her friends. Biddy asked them how they got free. Many had been born into freedom. Others had escaped slavery. But running off wasn't Biddy's way of doing things. She was going to *earn* her freedom.

Robert Smith had his own plan, though. Biddy and her daughters were his valuable property. They were an asset worth a hefty chunk of cash, money that could help him with his new life in California. He decided to take his slaves back to slave country and sell them at a profit. In December 1855 Smith told Biddy that her traveling days were far from over. He told her she had more walking to do—that she and her family were to follow him to Texas, a slave state, where he would cash them in.

But while Smith had been mapping out his plan, Biddy had been taking action on hers. She looked Robert Smith in the eye and refused flat out. Biddy had become acquainted with Lizzie Flake Rowan and two free black men, Charles Owens and Manuel Pepper. Lizzie, Charles, and Manuel were well versed in California state laws. They presented a petition to Judge Benjamin Hayes, asking that Biddy and her daughters be allowed to remain in California as free people. Judge Hayes accepted the petition right away. He prepared legal papers that spelled out freedom for Biddy, Biddy's children, and thirteen other Smith slaves. This was the ticket Biddy needed to be free forever. This was how she *earned* her freedom.

With the help of Charles Owens and Manuel Pepper, Biddy presented Robert Smith with an order requiring him to appear before a judge in the federal district court in Los Angeles. These legal papers made it clear to Smith that Biddy Mason—and all of his slaves—were now residents of California, and as such, they were free men and women.

When the court day came, Smith never showed up. The judge conducted two days of hearings, during which Biddy confirmed that Smith had indeed been her master for most of her life. On January 21, 1856, the judge declared Biddy and the other Smith slaves free.

Soon after Biddy had won her court case, her daughter Ellen married Charles Owens in Los Angeles. Together Biddy and Charles worked to improve conditions for the black residents of the city and its surrounding areas.

Biddy found employment as a nurse and midwife with Dr. John S. Griffin. She drew on the skills she had gained as a plantation midwife and from the caretaking she had done while traveling west as part of

Robert Smith's wagon train. Her patients ranged from wealthy Californians to those who didn't have a penny to their names. Biddy served anyone who needed her help. She delivered hundreds of babies. Sometimes she used root and herb potions as part of her nursing practices. She gained a reputation as an innovative healer, and people sought her out.

For ten years Biddy saved whatever she could from the $2.50 she earned each day. In 1866 she had enough money to purchase a house on Spring Street in Los Angeles. Biddy was one of the first black women of her time to buy a home of her own in the United States. The house cost $250.

As a homeowner Biddy learned that real estate was a powerful commodity. By owning land she could help other black people find affordable places to live, housing that didn't discriminate on the basis of skin color.

So Biddy continued to save her money. She bought several plots of land where she built homes to rent to black families. Some believe that by the late 1800s Biddy Mason was the wealthiest African American woman in Los Angeles.

Biddy was also rich in her generosity. She once said, "If you hold your hand closed, nothing good can come in. The open hand is blessed, for it gives in abundance, even as it receives."

Biddy kept her hands wide open, always ready to give. When a homeless soul needed a place to live, Biddy graciously opened her home on Spring Street. When a neighborhood full of eager-to-learn children needed a place to build their school, Biddy donated one of her lots. The same was true for grocery stores, day-care centers, and churches. When someone was looking for a place to build, Biddy provided.

In 1872 Biddy held an important meeting at her home. She called together a small group of men and women, including Charles Owens, who, like herself, wanted a place to worship in Los Angeles. With the help of Biddy's insightful guidance and her understanding of the city's requirements for constructing new buildings, the group founded the Los Angeles First African Methodist Episcopal Church.

Biddy Mason's legacy still thrives in Los Angeles. On March 27, 1988, a proud group of three thousand citizens—which included Mayor Tom Bradley, the first African American to be elected mayor of the city—gathered to cheer the contributions Biddy Mason made to Los Angeles during her lifetime. They honored Biddy by unveiling a beautiful tombstone to mark her grave site.

Today Biddy Mason's memory stands as strong as the buildings that were built under her charge.

Harriet Tubman

Born: Dorchester County, Maryland • 1820 or 1821 (exact date unknown)
Died: Auburn, New York • March 10, 1913

*"There was one of two things I had a right to, liberty or death;
if I could not have one, I would have the other."*

NOBODY KNOWS THE EXACT YEAR Harriet Ross was born. But no one can forget the courage and determination she demonstrated in her lifetime.

Harriet was one of eleven children born to Harriet Green and Benjamin Ross, slaves on the Edward Brodas plantation on Maryland's Eastern Shore. She was named Harriet after her mother. But folks who knew Harriet and her family well called them by their nicknames. Harriet's mother was known as Old Rit. Her daddy was Old Ben. And most of the slaves on the Brodas land called Harriet Araminta, the name Harriet's parents called her when she was a babe in the cradle. Old Rit and Old Ben called their child Minty for short.

Harriet's master, Edward Brodas, was one of the meanest slave masters around. As soon as Harriet was old enough to pinch cotton, she was forced to work long, hard days. Brodas was big on making money. To bring in extra cash, he *rented* little Harriet to nearby plantations, to people who were nearly as mean as he was.

When Harriet was just five years old, her master hired her out to work for a family named Cook. At the Cooks', Harriet slept and ate with the family dog. Like a dog, Harriet had to fetch the muskrats that had been snagged in James Cook's rattraps. The traps were set at the edge of an icy riverbank. Cook forced Harriet to wade in the water, waiting for the traplines to catch an animal. That river water was *freezing* cold, which set deep in Harriet's bones. It left her with a vicious cough and fever that grew to measles and bronchitis. So James Cook sent Harriet back to the Brodas plantation, where Old Rit nursed little Minty back to health.

Master Brodas was a man of little sympathy. As soon as Harriet's cough cleared up, he rented her out again, to a woman who needed a caretaker for her baby. Diapering and cuddling a baby sure beat looking for muskrats, though a baby requires constant attention.

One morning after breakfast, Harriet, a child herself, couldn't keep her thoughts off a bowl of sugar lumps that rested on the kitchen table. When Harriet's mistress wasn't looking, Harriet snuck a lump of sugar onto her tongue. She'd never tasted sugar before, and for a moment that sweet crystal lump eased the harsh treatment Harriet had endured. But when the mistress caught Harriet, that sweetness turned bitter in a snap. Harriet's mistress came after her with a rawhide switch.

Harriet ran and ran, past houses and farms and trees, until she'd out-run the mistress and her switch. Tired and out of breath, Harriet settled into a pigpen, where a sow and her piglets lived. She stayed hidden for nearly a week.

But even the pigpen was not safe. Harriet had to fight off the sow for food scraps. She grew hungry and frightened, and with no place else to go, she went back to her mistress, who whipped her good. When the whipping was over, the mistress sent Harriet back to the Brodas plantation. There, Old Rit dressed Minty's wounds and comforted her.

While running from her mistress, Harriet had caught a glimpse of freedom for the first time. Though it was brief, that freedom tasted sweeter than a hundred lumps of sugar. And it was something Harriet craved more than anything.

Harriet knew escaping from slavery was dangerous. She had heard all kinds of stories about those who tried to flee to the North. The ones who got caught suffered horsewhip beatings, or worse. Some were sold away from their parents, wives, and children. Despite the risk of getting caught, Harriet dreamed of freedom. One night Old Ben showed Harriet the North Star, a twinkling light from the heavens that pointed north. She looked at the star and longed to go.

On an autumn day in 1835, fifteen-year-old Harriet was tending to her work on the Brodas plantation when she glanced off and saw a black man carefully sneaking away. Master Brodas's overseer spotted the man, too, and followed him. Harriet wasn't far behind. She wanted to see *how* and *if* the black man was going to be free. But the runaway got only as far as the town store before the overseer caught up with him. The overseer pulled out his whip.

Then the overseer saw Harriet. He ordered her to hold the man still so that he could give him a beating. Well, there was no way Harriet was going to assist in a black man's beating, and she told the overseer so. She blocked the overseer's way so the black man could run. This made the

realized, "There was one of two things I had a *right* to, liberty or death; if I could not have one, I would have the other; for no man should take me alive; I should fight for my liberty as long as my strength lasted; and when the time came for me to go, the Lord would let them take me."

Harriet couldn't come right out and tell people that she was going to escape, so she secretly said good-bye by quietly singing an old spiritual while she worked:

> *When that old chariot comes,*
> *I'm going to leave you,*
> *I'm bound for the promised land.*
> *Friends, I'm going to leave you.*

That night Harriet wrapped a salted slab of fish and a hunk of bread in a croker sack. She took one long look at the North Star. And she ran.

Once more the sweetness of freedom began to fill Harriet as twigs snapped beneath her eager feet. She headed toward Bucktown, where the white woman who was helping escaped slaves lived. The woman welcomed Harriet into her cabin and told her of a lady whose husband was a driver on the Underground Railroad.

By the next morning Harriet had found that lady's house. To her surprise, the lady handed her a broom and told her to sweep the stray leaves from the doorstep. Harriet worried that she'd been tricked back into slavery. Soon she realized that this lady had asked Harriet to take up the broom so that Harriet would look like just any slave woman doing her work and wouldn't arouse suspicion.

That night the woman's husband tucked Harriet under a blanket in the bed of his wagon. He piled a flour sack on top of Harriet to keep her hidden, and with the North Star shining up ahead, he drove Harriet toward freedom. This was Harriet's first ride on the Underground Railroad, a ride she would never forget.

In the morning the man showed Harriet how to make the rest of her trip on foot, by following the river. The trip was not easy. Harriet had to hide in salt sheds and empty barns during the day, and travel at night. She ran and ran, in the cold, under black skies covered with clouds that at times hid the North Star from her. But Harriet kept on running up the Eastern Shore toward Pennsylvania, where freedom lay, some ninety miles from the Brodas plantation.

Finally, on a morning in 1849, Harriet was *free.* "I looked at my hands to see if I was the same person now that I was free," she later said. "There was such glory over everything; the sun came like gold through the trees and over the fields, and I felt like I was in heaven."

But Harriet's joy was mixed with sadness. Though *she* had attained freedom, so many of her loved ones—Old Rit, Old Ben, and her brothers and sisters—were still enslaved. She prayed. "Oh dear Lord," she said, "I ain't got no friend but you. Come to my help, Lord, for I'm in trouble!"

Trouble never daunted Harriet Tubman. She summoned her wits, went to Philadelphia, and got herself a job cooking and scrubbing dishes in a hotel kitchen. The workdays were long and tedious. But Harriet didn't mind. She was earning money. And while lathering plates and glasses, she had time to think. Harriet planned a return to Maryland to rescue her family. But when, she asked herself, would be the right time to risk a return? She prayed for guidance.

While in Philadelphia Harriet learned of the Philadelphia Vigilance

Committee, an organization that helped slaves escape along the Underground Railroad. The Philadelphia Vigilance Committee was headed by James Miller McKim, a white minister, and William Still, a black man who had been born free in Pennsylvania. McKim and Still had a primary purpose: to help free as many enslaved people as possible.

Harriet and William Still became friends. Through Still, Harriet met many fugitive slaves. She asked them about their escapes, and gathered facts that would help her help others get to the promised land.

One night Harriet got word that her sister Mary was to be auctioned and sold into cotton country. Mary's husband, John Bowley, was a free black man who knew people in the Underground Railroad network. John had made arrangements for Mary, himself, and their two children to get from Cambridge, Maryland, to Baltimore. But they needed a brave soul to guide them safely from Baltimore to Pennsylvania.

When Harriet learned of this, she knew her prayer had been answered. *Now* was the perfect time to go back along the Underground Railroad's trail. With the help of a Quaker family, Harriet's sister, John Bowley, and their children made it to the house of a kind white woman. Harriet was waiting there to greet them! Working her way from one Underground Railroad station to the next, Harriet guided her kin to Philadelphia—to the freedom she had found.

The rescue of her sister encouraged Harriet to go back to slave country again, to bring the rest of her family to the North. In the spring of 1851 Harriet returned to Maryland, where she rescued one of her brothers and two other men. She was putting her life on the line. But to Harriet a life without service to others was a life half lived.

In December 1851 Harriet returned to the Brodas plantation to get her husband, John. Going back to Brodas land was a scary prospect for Harriet. People there knew her and could spot her instantly.

Harriet hoped that John Tubman had changed his ways and would come with her to Pennsylvania. But on the bone-chilling night when Harriet knocked on the door of John's cabin, he met her with a smirk and told her he wasn't going anywhere. Harriet didn't waste her trip, though. She left the Brodas plantation with several slaves in her care.

Harriet now traveled twice a year, once in the spring and once in the fall. And with each trip, she learned something new that could help her

camouflage those she had rescued, and help her move quickly along the Underground Railroad. Over time she came to know every ditch, swamp, empty barn, and potato hole for hiding. She went to any length to help others. Once, she and a group of fugitives even hid in a heap of cow manure.

Harriet was beginning to get herself a reputation among slaves and slave owners who lived along Maryland's Eastern Shore. Black folks called her Moses. Like the Bible's Moses, she led her people to freedom. Plantation owners called Harriet *trouble*. They posted signs promising a $12,000 reward for anyone who captured "the woman called Moses."

Harriet now had to be extra cautious in her rescue missions. She had a price on her head. White slave catchers who saw her would most likely kill her instantly. This didn't stop Harriet. She returned to the South again and again. In 1857 she made one of her most meaningful escape missions. She finally rescued Old Rit and Old Ben. Because her parents had grown elderly and were too old to travel on foot, Harriet had been waiting for just the right time to take them to freedom. One night she broke into a stable on the Brodas plantation, hitched a horse to a wagon, hid her parents in the back of the wagon, and dashed off.

By the end of the following year, Harriet had led to freedom more than three hundred enslaved people. And her capture was now worth $40,000!

On January 1, 1863, President Abraham Lincoln issued the Emancipation Proclamation, a document that called for the freedom of all slaves. There was no further need for the Underground Railroad. Black people could travel freely anywhere they wished.

Years after the Underground Railroad's network ceased, Harriet recounted her work as one of the railroad's fearless conductors. She said, "I never ran my train off the track, and I never lost a passenger." Harriet Tubman's name will never lose its distinction. She has found her place as one of the greatest freedom seekers who has ever lived.

Ida B. Wells-Barnett

Born: Holly Springs, Mississippi • July 16, 1862
Died: Chicago, Illinois • March 25, 1931

"The price of liberty is eternal vigilance."

WHEN IDA B. WELLS-BARNETT was a girl, she was what folks down Mississippi way call a woman-child—a girl who had to grow up quickly because of hurt and hardship.

Ida was born the eldest of seven children to Jim and Lizzie Wells. Lizzie and Jim were firm believers in education. They taught Ida that schooling went hand in hand with success. Jim was a trustee at Shaw University, an institution founded in Holly Springs, Mississippi, by the Freedmen's Aid Society, for the purpose of educating newly freed slaves of all ages. (The school was later named Rust College.) Lizzie and Ida attended classes together at Shaw. Even though Ida was younger than most of the students, she was smarter than many of them. She embraced her parents' appreciation for schooling and excelled at her studies.

When Ida was fourteen, her mother and father, and her baby brother,

Stanley, died of yellow fever, a nasty epidemic that raged through Memphis, Tennessee, and northern Mississippi.

The neighbor-folk, friends of Ida's parents, gathered to lend Ida a hand. They mapped out a plan to provide homes for each of the Wells children. But Ida was determined to keep her family together. In response to the kind offers made by her parents' friends, Ida said a gracious no-thanks.

To raise her family under one roof, young Ida would need to earn a solid living. She now had mouths to feed, bills to pay, and household chores that wouldn't quit.

One caring couple—people called them Brother and Sister Miller—gave Ida the guidance she needed to make grown-up decisions about her future. The Millers encouraged Ida to take the local teaching certification examination, which would enable her to work as a schoolteacher. Ida knew she had the smarts to pass the exam, but she was still a child—a child with pigtails and knee skirts. No school was going to hire a kid to head up a classroom.

Well, Sister Miller fixed that. She combed out Ida's braids and swept her hair into a lady 'do—a prim, pretty bun that made Ida look older. Then Sister Miller altered the long-skirted dresses that were hanging in the closet of Ida's mother. After Sister Miller put her sewing needle to work, Lizzie's dresses fit Ida perfectly.

Ida passed the teacher's examination and was offered a job teaching in a one-room schoolhouse six miles from home. Ida's mule took Ida to and from work. Once Ida was teaching, nobody questioned her age. She carried herself like she was grown. And she had a ladylike way about her, even when she rode her mule. While Ida taught school, her grandmother Peggy came to stay with Ida's younger brothers and sisters.

It pleased Ida that she was able to make her way in the world and that she could support her family. But then Grandmother Peggy suffered a stroke. Now Ida had no choice but to split up her brothers and sisters. She and her youngest sisters, Lillie and Annie, went to Memphis, Tennessee, to live with their aunt Fannie. The other children stayed in Mississippi, to live with their aunt Belle.

Ida was hired to teach in a country school in Woodstock, Tennessee. The job paid Ida a good salary, but Woodstock was ten miles outside of Memphis—too far for a mule ride. So Ida rode a train to work. She stayed in Woodstock during the week, and saw Annie and Lillie only on weekends.

By law, black train passengers were forced to ride in the train's smoking car, among the cigarette fumes. *Whew*, that smoking car sure smelled *nasty*. Its stale air was hard to breathe. The smoke was as thick as intolerance. Ida soon grew sick and tired of the second-class treatment she suffered on the trains. She promised herself that someday she'd fight to change the unfair traveling conditions.

That day came on May 4, 1884, when Ida returned to Woodstock after visiting her sisters in Memphis. Ida decided to settle herself on the train in the first-class ladies' coach car—the whites-only car—among the nonsmokers. When the conductor tried to force her out of her seat, she refused to move. And when the conductor yanked Ida by the arm, she bit his hand! Even when the conductor called over his friends, who *all* tried to move Ida, Ida resisted. Finally, the men dragged Ida—schoolbooks and all—toward the smoking car. But Ida wasn't having it. As the train neared the first station stop, Ida gathered her belongings. When the train came to a halt, she quickly got off.

But Ida's trip was far from over. Her journey as a freedom fighter had just begun. With the help of a lawyer, Ida launched a civil rights case against the Chesapeake & Ohio Railroad. She won her case, and the court awarded her $500. Even though the state supreme court later reversed the decision, saying that Ida's behavior on the train warranted harassment by the conductor, Ida's legal battle was a small victory.

Ida finally landed a well-paying teaching job in Memphis. She was now a grown woman. Her brothers and sisters were grown, too, and no longer needed Ida to care for them. This was the first time since Ida's parents had died that she was free to seek out activities that were *fun*. Ida had more time to write in her diary, to reflect on the childhood that had escaped her, and to think about the years that lay ahead.

Ida joined a literary club that published a news journal called the *Evening Star*. The club met each Friday in the Vance Street Christian Church. Boy, that club sure made Ida happy. The men and women in the club were Ida's age. Many, like Ida, were teachers who loved reading, writing, lively talk, and hot-as-blazes debate. The *Evening Star* struck a special chord in Ida. Its intentions were the same as Ida's had been when she had refused to sit in a railroad car full of cigarette smoke: to speak out and breathe freely under the haze of racism.

Ida soon learned that newspapers were an excellent way to carry a message of strength to many people at once. She was appointed editor of the *Evening Star*, and she continued her work as a teacher while working for the newspaper in the evenings and on weekends. Ida viewed the *Evening Star* as a beacon that lit the darkness of bigotry. Through the articles she wrote, she could illuminate acts of discrimination and, at the same time, provide hope that prejudice would someday end.

Several African American newspapers reprinted Ida's articles, and soon people came to know Ida by her pen name, Iola. Ida was a skilled journalist, whose writings spoke the truth. Ida's writing made people think. And she knew that the best way to make people *act* was to push them to the boiling point. Her tell-it-like-it-is approach to writing was one of the many reasons the National Press Association named Ida the "princess of the press."

As any true princess would, Ida made some regal moves to suit her status. In 1889 the Colored Press Association elected Ida as their

secretary. That same year Ida purchased a one-third share of the *Memphis Free Speech and Headlight,* a weekly newspaper owned by two men, J. L. Fleming and Reverend Taylor Nightingale, the pastor for one of the largest black churches in Memphis. Ida served as editor of the *Free Speech.* And she kept on teaching. She eventually gave up her position as editor of the *Evening Star* to focus her attention on her work for the *Free Speech.*

The inferior conditions of black schools in Memphis had bothered Ida for a long time. Most black schools were in poor parts of town, with shabby classrooms and raggedy books. And in some schools even the teachers were second-rate, with no more education than the students themselves. Ida revealed these unfair conditions in an article for the *Free Speech.*

Ida's article caused an angry stir. Many didn't like the way Ida exposed the ugly realities of black schools. It was easier for many people to let educational injustices continue, pretending they did not exist. As a result of the article, Ida was fired from her teaching job. "But I thought it was right to strike a blow against a glaring evil and I did not regret it," Ida later said.

Fortunately Ida had saved money from her work as a teacher. She bought Reverend Nightingale's share of the *Free Speech* and became two-thirds owner of the paper along with J. L. Fleming. Ida devoted herself fully to making the *Free Speech* a top-notch publication. She worked hard to fill the paper with articles that would inspire people to further the cause for equality. She even printed the newspaper on pink paper to make people take notice.

Then, in March 1892, a brutal lynching occurred that turned Ida's calling into a crusade.

Ida's good friend Thomas Moss and two other men, Calvin McDowell and Henry Stewart, owned a grocery store they called the People's Grocery Company. Their store was a black-owned business nestled in a small Memphis neighborhood near the streetcar tracks. The People's Grocery Company served black customers mostly, but everyone who needed groceries was welcome. The store was well stocked and clean, and those who worked there were courteous and helpful to their customers. And the prices were good.

Folks in Memphis came to appreciate all that the People's Grocery had to offer, and they shopped there regularly. But a white storekeeper named Barrett, whose grocery store was nearby, saw the People's Grocery Company as a threat to his business.

Back then, a black person could be shot, hung, hunted, or burned for no reason at all. That's what lynching was—killing an innocent person (often a black person) who was presumed guilty of breaking the law, without giving him or her a fair trial.

In the eyes of some white people, Thomas Moss, Calvin McDowell, and Henry Stewart had committed a horrible crime: They had succeeded in business and had posed a threat to a white-owned business. As punishment, an angry mob took the three store owners to an empty brickyard just outside the Memphis city limits and killed them. The lynchings happened on a night darker than the blackest tar, and they set a blaze on Ida's consciousness.

Ida wrote a front-page article for the *Free Speech,* condemning the city of Memphis and encouraging black people to leave town. She was on a mission to expose the cruelties of lynching—to choke it out of existence by reporting its horrors.

Ida *studied* lynching. She went to the places where lynchings had happened and spoke to anyone who'd witnessed them. She comforted bereaved wives and children while at the same time collecting details about the crimes. Sometimes those who'd done the lynching bragged about it. Ida put their words to paper to let readers see the violence for themselves.

Ida's lynching accounts came to the attention of T. Thomas Fortune and Jerome B. Peterson, who owned a newspaper called the *New York Age.* Fortune and Peterson were familiar with Ida's work and had reprinted in their newspaper several articles she had written. In 1892 they invited Ida to visit them in New York. Before she left Memphis, Ida wrote a provocative article for the *Free Speech,* tallying recent lynchings and challenging the myth that black men are prone to attack white women.

Ida's words enraged many readers. And while Ida was in New York, an angry mob destroyed the offices of the *Free Speech.* Every sheet of paper, every ink can, every printing press was destroyed. The windows and furniture were smashed, too. The vandals threatened the life of Ida's friend and business partner, J. L. Fleming. J. L. quickly left Memphis and never looked back. He wrote to Ida, warning her to stay away from Memphis forever, for fear that *she* would be lynched.

Ida took a job with the *New York Age,* but her antilynching crusade was far from over. Ida gathered all the facts she'd collected about lynching and wove them together in an extensive article for the *New York Age.* The article was published on June 7, 1892. In her writing, Ida held back nothing. She pointed to anyone who was guilty of participating in a lynching, and she cited the exact times and places the lynchings had unfolded. Thousands of copies were printed and circulated throughout the United States.

Soon Ida was called upon by civil rights groups to speak out against lynching. She traveled as far as England, Scotland, and Wales to win support in her fight to stop lynchings in America.

When a black postmaster was lynched in South Carolina in the spring of 1898, Ida went to the White House to present a petition to President William McKinley, asking that the federal government make a greater effort to seek out and punish lynchers. While in Washington, Ida also lobbied Congress to pass a bill that would provide reparations for the postmaster's widow, since the man had been a federal employee. Both the president and members of Congress told Ida that something would be done, but Ida quickly discovered that antilynching was not their priority. Ida kept up her fight, though. She was firmly committed to her charge.

Ida once said, "The price of liberty is eternal vigilance." Though Ida didn't achieve an end to lynching in her lifetime, the power of her pen never faltered. And her commitment to social justice never waned. For Ida B. Wells-Barnett, the price of liberty was a price worth paying.

Mary McLeod Bethune

Born: Mayesville, South Carolina • July 10, 1875
Died: Daytona Beach, Florida • May 18, 1955

*"Look every man straight in the eye and
make no apology to anyone because of…color."*

MOST BABIES ARE BORN with their eyes closed up tight, their lips puckered like a drawstring purse. But when Mary Jane McLeod slid from her mother's womb, her eyes were wide open and she let loose a newborn's holler that seemed to be shouting good news. At least that's what legend says. The midwife who delivered Mary told Patsy and Samuel McLeod, Mary's mother and father, that little Mary was a very special child. Indeed she was. For her whole life Mary looked the world in the face and let her voice be heard.

Mary grew up on a hilly parcel of land in Mayesville, South Carolina. Patsy and Samuel called their small farm the Homestead. They hadn't always been free, but once slavery ended, they grew their own grapevines and fig trees, and a whole mess of cash-crop cotton.

Their cabin wasn't much more than slats of wood on a plot of soil.

But the Homestead and the McLeod family—all nineteen of them—were grand in their hospitality. Not party-giving grand, but lending-a-hand grand.

Because of the McLeods' generosity, the Homestead came to be known as a resting place for ministers who were passing through town and for wayward travelers who needed a hot meal and shelter for the night. On Sundays folks from Mayesville often gathered at the Homestead to fill the air with prayers and worship singing, and to praise the heavens for another day.

Mary soon learned that voices joined in song gave people strength, whether they were the ones singing or the ones who just listened and swayed to the music.

When Mary was seven years old, a fine teacher-lady came to Mayesville. Emma Wilson was a black teacher who had good sense and a sturdy Bible. She started a school for black children, the Trinity Presbyterian Mission School, in a small church down the road from Mary's farm.

At Miss Emma's school, Mary studied reading, writing, arithmetic, and the holy words of the Lord's Good Book. Miss Emma's one-room class wasn't much more than some pews, where the students sat, and a pulpit, where Miss Emma stood, but these simple surroundings made no difference to Mary. She took well to book learning. The five-mile walk to school each day put a mean scuff on her copper-toed shoes, but it sure didn't scrape her spirit. The child *loved* school! Mary had more than a *nose* for books, she had a *soul* for them.

Mary had a soul for teaching others, too. When she was no more than eleven years old, Mary used her math smarts to help her daddy figure out how much money he should get at the cotton gin for the crop pickin's he plunked down on the gin-man's scale. She showed people who couldn't read or write how to price the vegetables they sold in town, how to read the labels on the goods that were stocked at the village store, and how to count their pocket change. Before long, word spread through Mayesville that Samuel and Patsy McLeod had themselves a child who was blessed with the reading and writing gift.

In 1887, a year after she graduated from Miss Emma's school, Mary won a scholarship to the Scotia Seminary, a black women's school in Concord, North Carolina. The Scotia Seminary wasn't just *any* school. It was a boarding school for serious studying. A school that cost money to attend. A school for the best and brightest students.

Mary was twelve years old when she left the Homestead to attend Scotia. Her ambition was higher than Scotia's main hall, a three-story brick building. Her desire to learn new things was as fresh as the trees and flowers that graced Scotia's campus.

Mary missed her family and friends. She couldn't afford to travel to Mayesville to visit. But with all there was to learn at the seminary— history, geography, oration, and Bible studies—Mary kept busy. Some days there just wasn't time for looking back.

Even with Mary's hectic schedule, there was always time for prayer (that's something Mary learned back at the Homestead—prayer was a priority). Mary often settled herself in the little chapel at Faith Hall, Scotia's second brick building. Praying there made her feel closer to home somehow.

Mary's teachers said aside from being smart, she had a special call- ing—she could inspire people with her strong, steady voice. She was the best speaker in her class, and, boy, could she ever sing! Anybody who lis- tened to Mary deliver a speech or a hymn was deeply moved. Her voice was full and hefty, like her stature.

During her seven years at Scotia, Mary trained to achieve her deep- down wish to teach others about Christianity through missionary work, through spreading the Lord's word. More than anything, Mary wanted to travel to Africa, where she could share her religious beliefs with African people. But to do this, she needed more schooling.

Shortly before Mary was to graduate from Scotia, she applied to the mission school of the Moody Bible Institute in Chicago, Illinois. Once again Mary was blessed with a scholarship. And in July 1894 she began her studies in the largest city she'd ever seen.

Chicago was a far cry from the Homestead. The Moody Bible Institute was bigger than Miss Emma's church school and Scotia Seminary School combined. There were a thousand students at Moody, and Mary was the only black one among them. Some of the students were ignorant about black people. One girl thought Mary's skin was black from dirt! With all of her dignity, Mary pointed to a nearby vase of flowers and said, "Look at all the different colors…God made man just the way he made flowers. Some one color, some another, so that when they are gathered together, they make a beautiful bouquet."

Mary had the gift of finding just the right words, delivered with respect and kindness for others. During her study to become a missionary, Mary preached on the streets of Chicago to people who were down on their luck or just needed a little boost in their spirits. She visited jails, slum houses, and hospitals, where she offered comfort and inspiration by leading people in prayer or singing a hymn.

Mary could hardly wait to finish her studies at Moody; they would qualify her to carry out missionary work in Africa. But soon after graduation, in 1895, Mary was saddened to find there were no jobs for missionaries in Africa.

Disappointed, she went back to Mayesville to teach at Miss Emma's school—to give back to the school that had given her so much. A year later Mary found a teaching job at the Haines Normal and Industrial Institute, a school for black children in Augusta, Georgia. At Haines she taught more than book lessons; her students learned what Mary's parents had taught her: *Give freely.*

Mary took her students to nearby shantytowns, where they gave baths to poor children, wrapped them in clean towels, and combed their hair.

The following year Mary was transferred to the Kindell Institute in Sumter, South Carolina. She taught the students at Kindell the same lessons in human kindness.

Mary joined the choir of the local Presbyterian church, where she met a teacher named Albertus Bethune. Albertus fell in love with Mary's strong faith and her firm belief in the power to do right. He proposed to her, and they married. Mary soon gave birth to their only child, a boy named partly after his daddy and partly for Mary's kin: Albertus McLeod Bethune Jr.

Mary was beginning to make a name for herself. People were starting to hear about the teacher from Mayesville, South Carolina, who taught lessons that couldn't be found in an eye-high stack of textbooks. The pastor of a Presbyterian school in Palatka, Florida, had heard of Mary's teaching methods. Soon after Albertus was born, the pastor invited Mary to teach at his church school.

Mary accepted the job. She brought a fresh outlook to the Palatka school. She hired new instructors and showed them her ways of teaching. As the school grew, a small wish sparked up inside of Mary: *I wish I could start my own school.* Now, anybody knows that *wishing* and *doing* are two different things. And Mary McLeod Bethune wasn't just one of those sapheaded daydreamers. She was a *doer.* All she needed was a mustard seed of inspiration.

In 1904 Mary heard about a railroad, the Florida East Coast Railway, being built along the Atlantic Coast to Daytona Beach, Florida. All kinds of folks—black folks, mostly—headed to Florida to find work on the rails. The men dug ditches and laid tracks; the women scrubbed laundry and scaled fish for eating.

Grown people had plenty of work to keep them busy. But their children wandered among the rubble, making toys out of scrap metal and stone. Those kids needed schooling! But there were no grade schools for black children in Daytona Beach.

That was all the seed Mary needed. On October 4, 1904, Mary McLeod Bethune opened the Daytona Normal and Industrial Institute for Negro Girls, the school she had founded. It was the first grade school for black children in the community, and one of the few of its kind anywhere.

Mary's school was a bare-bones cottage near the train tracks. At first only five girls came to Mary's school. Then a slew of kids, including boys, started flocking in.

Many of the children's mothers worked as maids for rich white folks who went away—with their maids—for long vacations. Mary took the maids' children in as her own. She housed them, fed them, taught them, prayed with them, raised them. Just as in the other schools where Mary had been a teacher, here her students learned the importance of generosity. She also taught them crafts and homemaking, so that they could earn a good living when they were grown.

Mary was always thinking of thrifty ways to supply her school. She used pieces of burnt wood for chalk. Packing crates were used for desks. Mary made pen ink from elderberry juice. Those students who lived at the school slept on corn sacks that Mary had stuffed with Spanish moss.

And, oh, Mary's sweet-potato pies! Not a night went by when Mary wasn't mashing, rolling out, and baking up the sweetest pies ever. Not a morning passed that didn't find Mary riding her bicycle through town, selling her pies to raise funds for her school. Whenever anybody bought a pie from Mary, she told them all about the institute.

To help Mary, some of the townspeople donated fish from their day's catches. Others sent oranges from their groves, for the students to eat. Mary's students helped her earn money to keep the institute going by singing hymns on street corners.

In two years' time, Mary had 250 students. Her cottage classroom was much too small for all those eager-to-learn kids, so Mary rented a large hall to house her school. But the school just kept on *growing.* And so did Mary's seed of inspiration. Using every last penny she'd earned from selling her pies, Mary purchased a piece of land that was being used as a city dump. The men who worked along the railroad called the messy plot Hell's Hole. But to Mary's eyes the site was a whole lot of opportunity.

She and her students carted junk off the land. Rich people saw that Mary meant business. They donated money to Mary's cause, and soon she had enough to build a brick building large enough to house her entire student body. She had turned Hell's Hole into a haven for learning. Mary named the building Faith Hall, after her favorite prayer place at Scotia Seminary. Two mottoes hung over the main entrance to the hall: ENTER TO LEARN and DEPART TO SERVE.

Some children had been Mary's students since her school opened. They had grown with the institute as it went from a girls' elementary school to a high school, then to a junior college and to a college. By 1908 there were so many boys enrolled, Mary changed her school's name to the Daytona Educational Industrial Training School.

With her school, Mary had given her students something few black people had in the early 1900s—she'd given them the dignity of choice. With an education to lean on, they didn't have to take backbreaking jobs if they didn't want to. They could go north and find work as typists, clerks, and accountants.

This enraged some white people, especially those who had no schooling themselves. In 1920 during the elections for the mayor of Daytona, the Ku Klux Klan took its anger out on Mary and her students. Of the two men running for mayor, the Klan's favorite was the one who was against black people having their own schools. The other candidate supported Mary's vision. He saw the value in her school. He also promised to fix the streets and lampposts in the black part of town if he was elected.

Mary had spent the summer helping black people register to vote and encouraging them to cast their ballots on Election Day. This added fuel to the Klan's anger. Its members threatened Mary—told her she'd better quit her campaign efforts, or else. But "Faith and courage, patience and fortitude" was Mary's brave creed. She told her students, "Use your minds…Don't be afraid of the Klan! Hold your head up high. Look every man straight in the eye and make no apology to anyone because of…color."

On the night before Election Day, the Ku Klux Klan marched onto the campus of Mary's school. They marched in an angry parade, mounted on horses, robed like ghosts. The Klansmen had turned off all the streetlights in Daytona, forcing the town into complete darkness. The black sky looked even darker against the Klan's torch: a burning cross. The Klan intended to frighten Mary and her students so that they would be too afraid to vote.

Well, the Klan could control the town's lights, but the electricity for Mary's school belonged to Mary. She spread word to her students to turn off all the lights in the main building and to flood the outside grounds with every light on campus.

Mary and her students stood nestled in darkness, watching from the window. But the Klan's idea had been turned back on them. Under the shining glare of the campus lights, Mary could see every last one of them!

Soon the Klan's horses grew ornery. With the lights blinding them, the Klansmen were caught. They left in a hurry. The next day, Mary went to the polling site to help black people vote. Her candidate of choice won the election. And Mary won even more support for her school.

In time the Daytona Educational Industrial Training School became the pride of Daytona Beach. New students just kept on coming. And once again the place started to put on too much meat for its joints. Then, in 1923, Mary's school joined up with Cookman Institute, a nearby men's college. The combined schools became the Bethune-Cookman Collegiate Institute. Mary was its proud president. Her seed of inspiration had blossomed into a towering tree of accomplishment.

But Mary wanted to keep growing. She believed that black women who came together for a common cause were a "steady, uplifting, and cleansing influence" on the struggles black people faced.

To put this "steady influence" into practice, Mary formed the National Council of Negro Women (NCNW) in 1935. The Council spoke out against lynching—one of the ugliest crimes committed against black men. And the group fought for the rights of women from as far away as the Philippines and as close as Philadelphia.

By this time America had slipped into what was called the Great Depression. Times were hard; there weren't many jobs. Formerly rich folks and poor folks, black folks and white folks, stood together in the same unemployment lines.

President Franklin D. Roosevelt worked to put an end to the Depression. He called on Mary to help him. In 1936 the president named Mary the director of the Division of Negro Affairs, a department that was part of the National Youth Administration, in Washington D.C. Mary's job was to seek out young black people in the fields and backstreets of America, and help them find employment. No black woman had ever been in charge of a federal agency. Mary carried out her post with the same commitment that she'd brought to her work as a teacher.

She became good friends with Eleanor Roosevelt, the president's wife. They spent many hours together talking about ways to improve conditions for African Americans. Sometimes when people saw the two women together, they would say, "There's Eleanor Roosevelt, the first lady. And there's Mary McLeod Bethune, a lady of firsts."

Ella Josephine Baker

Born: Norfolk, Virginia • December 17, 1903
Died: New York City • December 13, 1986

"Sit-ins and other demonstrations are concerned with something much bigger than a hamburger or even a giant-sized Coke."

As a little girl, Ella Baker was blessed with sass, smarts, and a whole lot of strength. Ella came from a family of determined people. When slavery was abolished, Ella's grandfather Ross, who had been enslaved, saved enough money to buy himself several acres of land. This was land he'd slaved on for years before freedom came.

Ross was a proud, defiant minister, who spoke out against prejudice. His wife, Josephine Elizabeth, after whom Ella was named, also held her head high in the face of indignity. When Josephine had been enslaved, her mistress chose a husband for her, some man she didn't truly love. Josephine wanted to marry Ross, and against her mistress's wishes, she did.

Ella's grandparents loved to share these stories of courage with Ella. Some say Ella got her sassy spirit and her strength from Josephine and Ross.

out like never before. For Ella New York represented a chance to use her college education and her Baker-family resolve to help others.

When Ella arrived in New York, she was immediately struck by the poverty she saw on the city's streets. This encouraged her to attend political meetings and rallies. She joined the Young Negroes Cooperative League (YNCL), a group that organized cooperative grocery stores throughout the United States. She was active with the Works Progress Administration (WPA), a government program that provided jobs for unemployed laborers and artists. And she worked with several women's rights groups, such as the Women's Day Workers and Industrial League, a union for domestic employees.

Ella also wrote articles for various newspapers, including the *West Indian News* and the *National News*. In 1935 Ella contributed to an investigative report that exposed the poor working conditions of black domestic workers in New York City. The article was published in the *Crisis,* the magazine of the National Association for the Advancement of Colored People (NAACP), whose headquarters were in New York City.

In 1938 Ella took a job with the NAACP, where she could fight against racial injustice and fight to clip Jim Crow's wings once and for all. Her first job there was as an assistant field secretary. She traveled throughout the South for months at a time, explaining the NAACP's mission and recruiting new members.

But Jim Crow was still alive and well in the South, and many black folks weren't so eager to join any cause that would disgruntle white people. White people owned most of the businesses that kept the South going. They were the ones hiring, and they were also the ones who, at the snap of a finger, could fire any black man or woman they thought was becoming too outspoken.

To make matters worse, the lynching of innocent black people had become widespread in the South. Some accounts say nearly three thousand black people were lynched in the United States between the late 1800s and the 1930s. Getting laws passed that would stop lynching was at the top of the NAACP's list.

Many Southern blacks saw the NAACP as a bunch of uppity northerners. Many whites saw them as black people who were overstepping their bounds. To Ella the NAACP was hope for putting an end to the racial discrimination that plagued the nation and endangered the lives of black people. But she had to work hard—and sometimes talk fast—to get her point across before some intolerant soul tried to shush her.

Ella once said, "If you talk down to people, they can sense it. They can *feel* it. And they know whether you are talking *with* them or *at* them, or talking *about* them." She knew that the best way to reach people was to speak to them as she would a friend. And she had an easygoing way about her that drew people in. She was far from uppity, and over time she gained the trust of people who once had been doubters of the NAACP's importance. Thanks to Ella, the NAACP's membership grew.

In 1942 the NAACP appointed Ella the national director of branches. It was her job to manage all the local NAACP offices in the United States. The NAACP believed that to grow strong it had to plant firm roots in the towns and cities that dotted the nation. Local NAACP offices, which spread from Tallahassee to Topeka to Pepperdine, were the seeds that set these roots to spreading. Most branch offices were in black neighborhoods. Ella helped each branch seek out new members, and she advised them on how to approach city officials when they wanted to improve things like housing conditions and hiring practices.

Through Ella's efforts with the NAACP, black people began to see that together they could make a change. And in 1954 when Ella became president of the NAACP New York City branch, that torch she had lit glowed even brighter. As branch president, Ella took a special interest in school segregation. Black people were dead-tired of Jim Crow, yet he hovered over every school yard and classroom, preventing black students and white students from learning under the same roof.

During an NAACP visit to Alabama, Ella made a friend named Rosa Parks. Rosa was a member of the NAACP and the secretary of the Montgomery branch. She was the catalyst that launched the Montgomery, Alabama, bus boycott.

The Montgomery bus boycott was an important step in gaining equality for African Americans. The boycott ended segregation on buses in the state of Alabama. Ella helped sponsor several fund-raising events that kept the boycott going. But there were still more battles to win. To Ella, and to many other black people, there remained a long journey ahead. A journey that required even more of what Ella Baker did best: push people into action.

Soon after the Montgomery bus boycott, civil rights crusader Martin Luther King Jr. called together the South's leading black ministers to attend a meeting in Atlanta, Georgia, on January 11, 1957. With racial tensions building, the South was in a sorry state of hatred. On the eve of the meeting, several Montgomery churches were bombed. Dr. King went to Montgomery to comfort the sufferers, leaving Ella and his wife, Coretta Scott King, to coordinate the meeting in his absence. Civil rights activists

Bayard Rustin and Reverend Fred Shuttlesworth worked with Ella and Coretta to pull the meeting together. The sixty ministers who gathered in Atlanta formed the Southern Christian Leadership Conference (SCLC), a civil rights group made up of church congregations and freedom fighting organizations throughout the South.

Dr. King was president of the SCLC. He asked Ella to organize the SCLC's Crusade for Citizenship, a voter registration campaign that encouraged black people to vote. Ella went right to work, planning twenty-two rallies in twenty-two Southern cities, scheduled to happen on February 12, 1958. Organizing the rallies was only part of the job. To make the crusade a success, Ella had to convince black people that voting was their right—and the right way to fight for change. The rallies took place as planned, but not many black people registered to vote.

Then, on February 1, 1960, four black college students in Greensboro, North Carolina, struck out against segregation by sitting at a Woolworth's lunch counter reserved for whites only. When the waitress refused to serve them, they sat. When people called them names and cursed them, they sat. When their backsides ached and their feet fell asleep, they sat. They stayed at that lunch counter all day long, sitting for freedom. Their quiet demonstration became known as the Greensboro sit-in.

The next day, more students came to Woolworth's to sit, and even more came after that. Soon these sit-ins—top stories on the nightly news—spread through the South. The students endured all kinds of torment—hot coffee spilled on their heads; mustard squirted in their eyes; burning cigarettes pressed to their skin. But they didn't budge, and they held fast to their aim: to protest without violence.

Ella knew that the best way to make change happen was to get young people more involved in the civil rights movement. Young people were less concerned about the ways of whites. They had the courage it took to fuel the fire for justice.

These sit-ins were a boost to the struggle for equality. But Ella believed the students needed guidance and organization to make their sit-ins truly effective. To help the students coordinate their efforts, Ella devised a gathering, the Student Leadership Conference, in North Carolina, at Shaw University, where she had received her diploma.

The three-day conference took place in April 1960, during Easter weekend. Nearly three hundred students from all over the South came dressed in their best—Easter bonnets and bow ties—ready to share their ideas. During the conference, they formed the Student Nonviolent Coordinating Committee (SNCC).

Ella became SNCC's chief adviser. The students lovingly called her Miss Ella and considered her their guardian angel. She established SNCC's main office, in Atlanta, and helped the group define their slogan: "We are all leaders."

To keep the cause for equality pressing onward and to praise SNCC's mission, Ella wrote an article, which was published in June 1960, for the *Southern Patriot* newspaper. She wrote:

The Student Leadership Conference made it crystal clear that . . . sit-ins and other demonstrations are concerned with something much bigger than a hamburger or even a giant-sized Coke. . . . Negro and white students, North and South, are seeking to rid America of the scourge of racial segregation and discrimination—not only at lunch counters but in every aspect of life.

Ella Baker's unstoppable determination helped bring that fight for freedom alive.

Dorothy Irene Height

Born: Richmond, Virginia • March 24, 1912

"Black women are the backbone of every institution."

Dorothy height was a churchgoing child. When she was growing up, she and her parents worshiped every Sunday at the Baptist church in Rankin, Pennsylvania, the small mining town where they lived. Dorothy's father, James, was the church choirmaster. Her mother, Fannie, had a knack for organizing church club activities.

It was in church that young Dorothy learned the powers of preaching and the importance of drawing people together for a common cause. And it was from hearing many sermons that Dorothy discovered the beauties of a well-delivered speech. Even as a girl, Dorothy Height learned first-hand that the words *she* spoke—and the fortitude with which she spoke them—had the power to change people's lives.

When Dorothy was a student at Rankin High School, she won several speech contests. She became a finalist in a state oratory contest that was held in Harrisburg, Pennsylvania, the state capital. Before leaving

Rankin, Dorothy was encouraged by her mother to keep her head high and to speak from her heart.

Dorothy's Latin teacher and her school principal drove her to the contest finals in Harrisburg. During the drive, Dorothy held fast to her mother's advice. But it was hard to keep her head high when she was stopped at the door of the hotel where the contest was being held. It never occurred to them that Dorothy had come as a contest entrant. They took one look at the black child who stood before them and dismissed her without taking the time to ask why she'd come.

But Dorothy was there to speak her piece in front of the contest judges. She went back out to the car and changed into the special dress her mother had hung there for her. Then, despite the disrespect she'd faced, she went right into the contest.

Dorothy was the only black contest participant. And she was the last entrant to speak. All the judges were white. Still, she gave a rousing speech about the importance of peace among people. Then she added a special message to her speech. She recounted the story of Jesus' birth and told everyone that just as Mary and Joseph could not get into the inn on that special night, she, too, had been shunned by the people at the hotel—but *she* was denied because of her skin color.

The contest judges awarded Dorothy first prize.

After her victory in Harrisburg, Dorothy went on to win a one-thousand-dollar scholarship in a national oratorical contest sponsored by the Elks Fraternal Society. With her prize money and the straight As she'd earned at Rankin High School, Dorothy enrolled in New York University in 1929.

Dorothy had what some people call double-time smarts. At New York University she gave new meaning to the term *higher learning*. She earned a bachelor's degree in social work *and* a master's degree in educational psychology—completing both in four years!

Like her mother, Fannie, Dorothy had a knack for working with people. Soon after she graduated from college, Dorothy got a job at the New York City Department of Welfare, where she was a caseworker. At the welfare department, Dorothy learned the best ways to resolve conflicts and to show people how to work together peacefully.

Dorothy's talents for helping people get along with one another were especially useful in the spring of 1935, when a Harlem teenager was roughed up by white store clerks who saw him shoplift a pocketknife. The incident sparked a series of race riots, which spread their fury through Harlem. City officials who knew of Dorothy's work with the welfare department called on Dorothy right away. She was one of the first African Americans they chose to map out a plan for ending the unrest in Harlem.

Dorothy knew that Harlem was just one of many places in the United States in which young people struggled to have their voices heard by the U.S. government. While working to stop the riots, she became one of the young leaders of the National Youth Movement, a government initiative to provide job training and counseling for young people.

The National Youth Movement was a program founded as part of President Franklin D. Roosevelt's plan to help America come out of the Great Depression. The president's plan was known as the New Deal. The New Deal brought hope to many Americans. It was a time of change, a time when people began to look toward a bright future for the United States. Eleanor Roosevelt, the first lady, added an important dimension to the New Deal. She worked to improve the rights of women and black people. This inspired Dorothy.

During the late 1930s, while the New Deal was in full swing, Dorothy worked to stop segregation. She used her gift of eloquence to speak out against lynching and to voice her views about the unfair treatment of black people by the courts. Dorothy's speeches didn't bring about an immediate end to lynching or an instant change in the court system, but her willingness to speak out against these evils did help put positive changes in motion.

In 1937 Dorothy was appointed assistant director of the Harlem Young Women's Christian Association (YWCA). This job changed Dorothy's life forever. On November 7, 1937, Mary McLeod Bethune, founder and president of the National Council of Negro Women (NCNW), held an important NCNW meeting at the Harlem YWCA.

Eleanor Roosevelt attended the meeting, where she was to be the honored speaker of the day. It was Dorothy's responsibility to escort Mrs. Roosevelt into the auditorium and to usher her out when the meeting ended. While Dorothy was leaving the auditorium with Mrs. Roosevelt, Mary McLeod Bethune took notice of the professional manner with which Dorothy accompanied the first lady. She approached Dorothy, asked her her name, and urged her to become an NCNW member.

Dorothy didn't have to think twice about Mrs. Bethune's offer. The NCNW stood for everything Dorothy believed in: fair employment, fair pay, and fair schooling for black women. She joined the National Council of Negro Women right away.

While taking an active role as an NCNW volunteer, Dorothy continued her work with the YWCA and with the young people of Harlem. Just one year after meeting the first lady, Dorothy became one of ten Americans to help Eleanor Roosevelt organize the World Youth Congress, a meeting to examine the issues of young people, held at Vassar College, in Poughkeepsie, New York.

But Dorothy didn't limit herself to work among politicians and those people with college educations. She was a civil rights supporter for anyone who needed her help. In 1938 she became an advocate for the many young black women who worked as domestics in New York City. She spoke before the New York City Council about the demeaning conditions black women in Brooklyn and the Bronx had to endure to earn a living.

She addressed the council with the same articulateness that had won her so many speech contests. She said that the streets of New York City had become a "slave market." She told the council about how black girls had to flag down white people driving by in their cars, then bargain with them for a day's housework at dirt cheap wages. She implored the council to help bring an end to this practice and to provide better work opportunities for black women.

The battle for better work opportunities and fair wages was a long one. Change took time. But rather than wait for the New York City Council to take action, Dorothy showed the domestic workers how to help themselves by forming their own unions. These unions would make sure the women were paid fairly and were working under fair conditions.

Some say Dorothy Height didn't have one tired bone in her body. She kept on keeping on, all in the name of helping black women gain equality. Putting her shoulder to the wheel of *one* organization wasn't enough for Dorothy. She helped pave the way to equal rights by steering several causes.

Dorothy's volunteer work with the NCNW was an ongoing commitment that she never let rest. The same was true of her work with the YWCA. In 1939 she moved to Washington, D.C., to serve as the executive secretary of the YWCA Phillis Wheatley Home. She later became a member of the national board of the YWCA, where she held many leadership positions until she retired from her YWCA work in 1977.

When Dorothy first arrived in Washington, D.C., in 1939, Mary McLeod Bethune wasted no time putting her to work for the National

Council of Negro Women. Dorothy served as the executive secretary. This position allowed her to learn from Mary McLeod Bethune's ability to rally for equal rights and to gain support from important government officials, the way she'd done with Eleanor Roosevelt.

While in Washington, Dorothy also became a member of Delta Sigma Theta Sorority, Inc. Soon after she joined Delta Sigma Theta, Dorothy launched a national Delta project.

She called her sorority sisters together to examine why black women were excluded from so many of the jobs that were open to white women. This project went far beyond finding jobs for black people. Dorothy helped get black women appointed to positions of leadership in the organizations that set policy for workers in America. In 1947 Delta Sigma Theta elected Dorothy as their national president, an appointment that she kept until 1956.

Leadership always suited Dorothy well. When called to a post of authority, Dorothy fit herself to the task without flinching. In 1957, shortly after her presidential duties with Delta Sigma Theta ended, she assumed the presidency of the National Council of Negro Women.

Dorothy was NCNW's fourth president. She proudly carried the torch Mary McLeod Bethune lit for her. Under Dorothy's leadership, the NCNW became a solid civil rights force—an organization that made folks take notice of the power black women command when they're gathered together in the name of justice.

And, boy, did people take notice of all the things Dorothy did as NCNW president. When she started a series of food drives sponsored by the NCNW, people noticed. When the NCNW set up programs to find housing for needy families, people noticed. And when Dorothy led the

NCNW in establishing the Fannie Lou Hamer Day Care Center in Ruleville, Mississippi, people couldn't *help* but notice.

And Dorothy didn't stop there. During her tenure as NCNW president, she began to raise funds to build a statue of Mary McLeod Bethune in a federal park in Washington, D.C. Even with Dorothy's fortitude and outspokenness, this was no easy feat. Raising the thousands of dollars needed to erect the statue was only one small step in the process. Dorothy met tremendous resistance from people who felt that the money she'd earned for the statue could be better used to help the cause for civil rights.

Dorothy had to present to Congress her intentions for building the statue. To her way of thinking, erecting a monument to Mary McLeod Bethune, one of America's most distinguished black leaders, was an important means of inspiring people to act on behalf of African Americans. Dorothy had to work through five sessions of Congress and four presidents to gain approval for the Mary McLeod Bethune monument. But she never gave up. In 1974 the Bethune memorial statue became the first monument to an African American erected in a public park in Washington, D.C.

Dorothy often has been the only woman in the company of men speaking out for black justice. In 1962 a group of black leaders, all of them men, came together to discuss the civil rights concerns of black Americans. The group called themselves the United Civil Rights Leadership. It was composed of several civil rights luminaries, including Dr. Martin Luther King Jr. Dorothy represented the voice of black women through the National Council of Negro Women. Like many equal rights organizations of the time, the United Civil Rights Leadership had a similar goal: to carry on the crusade for human rights.

Dorothy encouraged the group to invite young people to their meetings, to gain fresh insight into the civil rights struggle by giving students a chance to express their ideas for helping the cause.

Dorothy once said, "Black women are the backbone of every institution, but sometimes they are not recognized as even being there, even in the civil rights movement."

Thankfully, Dorothy Height's commitment to racial equality has given black women an undeniable presence on the face of American justice.

Rosa Parks

Born: Tuskegee, Alabama • February 4, 1913

"The only tired I was, was tired of giving in."

ROSA MCCAULEY WAS NAMED after her maternal grandmother, Rose Edwards. The name fit her perfectly. She was a beautiful, delicate child, who was always blossoming with enthusiasm. Rosa's father, James McCauley, worked as a carpenter. He traveled through the South building homes. Rosa saw very little of her father while she was growing up. His work kept him away from his family for long periods of time.

Rosa's mother, Leona, was a schoolteacher who settled with her children in Pine Level, Alabama, the place where she was raised. Rosa and her baby brother, Sylvester, lived on an eighteen-acre farm with their mother and their grandparents, Grandma Rose and Grandpa Sylvester.

Because there were so few black schools in the immediate community, Leona often traveled to other towns to find teaching assignments. She also earned money by styling hair for the women in Pine Level and by mending clothes for neighbors and friends.

Although Rosa missed having her father nearby, she loved living with her grandparents. Grandpa Sylvester was an outspoken man, who was solid in his convictions. He believed that no human being had just cause to mistreat another, and that if somebody did you wrong, you should not stand for it.

From a very young age, Rosa learned about racial hatred. Both her grandparents had been slaves. They told her many stories about the wicked treatment black people had endured at the hands of white slave masters. But even though slavery had ended by the time Rosa was born, she still experienced the oppression of racism firsthand. This bigotry was evident mostly in laws that demanded separate schools, drinking fountains, restaurants, and public bathrooms for black people and white people.

When Rosa was six, she began to attend Pine Level's only black school, a shabby one-room schoolhouse where students from first through sixth grades crammed together on benches. There were no desks, no windows, a handful of tattered books, and one teacher for fifty kids. During the winter, the sixth-grade boys had to build a fire in a woodstove to keep the classroom warm.

The school for white students was a place black children could only dream about. It was made of bricks. It had a playground. There were books galore. There were plenty of teachers. And there was lots of heat. It wasn't fair that the amenities that made the white schools so fine were purchased with public tax money that came from the pockets of both Pine Level's white *and* black residents.

Leona saved every penny she could, and when Rosa was eleven years old, her mother sent her to the Montgomery Industrial School for Black

Girls, a private school in Montgomery, Alabama. During the school year, Rosa lived with her aunt Fannie. At her new school Rosa learned everything, from how to read world maps to how to mix remedies for sick and ailing souls. She even took cooking lessons.

But a private education couldn't shield Rosa from the public humiliation of racism that was common in the South in the 1920s. Rosa often rode streetcar trolleys to school—segregated streetcars in which she, along with every other black rider, was forced to sit in the back.

When Rosa was sixteen, her grandma Rose died. Soon after that Rosa's mother got sick. Rosa quit school and returned to Pine Level so that she could work to help support her family. She spent the final years of her childhood running the Edwards's farm and earning money cooking and sewing, two skills she had perfected at the Montgomery Industrial School.

In 1931 a neighbor introduced Rosa to Raymond Parks. Raymond was as dandy as they come. He was smart, smooth talking, forthright, and persistent. And he drove a red car that had a rumble seat in the back. Raymond was a barber who worked in downtown Montgomery. He took a quick liking to Rosa. But she was not immediately impressed with him. He came to Rosa's house several times to ask Rosa's mother if he could take Rosa for a drive in his car. It was clear to Leona that Raymond Parks was intelligent and sincere. She agreed to let him spend time with her daughter, but it was Rosa who kept turning down Raymond's offers.

Finally, when Rosa said yes to a short ride with Raymond, she saw that he was more than just a pretty boy with a flashy car. Like Rosa's grandfather, Raymond was a man of conviction. He was well-spoken and cared deeply about the plight of black people in the South. And he was an active member of the National Association for the Advancement of Colored People (NAACP).

The more Raymond told Rosa about his commitment to helping black people, the more Rosa's awareness grew. Her love for Raymond grew, too. In December 1932 Rosa McCauley and Raymond Parks were married, in Pine Level at the home of Rosa's mother. Rosa was nineteen years old.

Raymond knew that Rosa had been forced to quit high school to take care of her family. It troubled him that his wife had to give up something she enjoyed so much. Soon after Rosa and Raymond married, Raymond encouraged Rosa to complete her education. Rosa was happy to return to school. She graduated from Alabama State Teachers College in 1933, with a high school diploma.

Rosa found work as a helper at Saint Margaret's Hospital in Montgomery. At night she worked as a seamstress at home, mending and tailoring clothes. Rosa was grateful for her job, but going to work drove home the sad reality of segregation. When Rosa took the city bus to work, she had to go through the same degrading ritual day after day. She would step on the bus at the front and buy a ticket from the driver. Then she'd have to leave the bus, walk around to the back, and enter the bus again through the rear door. All black passengers had to sit in the back. Only white people were allowed to ride at the front of the bus. This was the law. If you were black and the back of the bus was too crowded, tough. You had to wait for the next bus, go through the same drill, and pray you would get to work on time.

Rosa was growing tired of this daily disgrace. Sometimes she would get onto the bus at the front and pay her fare, like always. Then before the driver had a chance to take full notice of her, Rosa would breeze through the front section of the bus to find her seat in the back.

Several drivers came to associate Rosa with her defiance. Once, in 1943, a driver kicked Rosa off his bus because she refused to enter the bus through the back door. He told Rosa that if she thought she was too high-and-mighty to follow the rules, she should find another bus to ride. But there *was* no other bus for her to ride. And there were no drivers bold enough to turn their backs on the ugly ways of discrimination.

As the wife of a civil rights activist (and the granddaughter of a civil rights believer), Rosa had learned three important things about changing the unjust treatment black people had suffered: Change takes time. Change takes strength. Change takes the help of others. Rosa Parks had all three.

She knew that one of the best ways to put these advantages to work would be to join the NAACP. But becoming an NAACP member wasn't as simple as it seemed. Rosa's husband didn't think it was a good idea. The NAACP existed under the constant threat of white vigilantes who looked for violent ways to sabotage group meetings. Sometimes NAACP meetings had to be held during late-night hours, in dark, secret places where Klansmen and the police couldn't find the group.

Raymond supported his wife's wish to stop segregation, but at the same time, he feared for her safety. And there were very few women enrolled as NAACP members. If Rosa were to join, she would be shrouded by the influence of men. Rosa respected her husband's concerns. But in 1943 when she spotted a picture in the *Alabama Tribune* of Johnnie Carr, a friend of hers from the Montgomery Industrial School, who was acting as a temporary secretary for the local NAACP Montgomery branch, Rosa knew she had to join. Soon after Rosa saw the newspaper article, she attended the annual NAACP Montgomery meeting. This was the meeting to elect new officers. There were sixteen people at the meeting—fifteen men and Rosa Parks.

When it came time to elect a permanent volunteer secretary, everybody looked to Rosa. They all figured secretarial work was women's work and she was the natural choice. Rosa accepted the job gladly. What better way to serve the cause than to document its progress?

Rosa wasted no time. She put her pen to paper right then and there, and recorded the remaining minutes of the meeting. From that day on for the next twelve years, Rosa took her position as the NAACP Montgomery chapter secretary very seriously. And when he saw the commitment that Rosa brought to her volunteer work, so did her husband.

Rosa organized branch meetings, kept the books, wrote and mailed letters and press releases, and at every turn, drummed up new members. When the office phone rang, Rosa answered it. When someone had a question about the workings of the branch, Rosa answered that, too.

As branch secretary, Rosa worked closely with E. D. Nixon, the chapter president. Under E. D.'s direction, she recorded all of the cases of discrimination and violence against black people in the state of Alabama. The cases seemed never ending. There were hundreds of them.

Documenting these cases showed Rosa that racism in Alabama was big. It was powerful. It gathered momentum with each mile it covered. It would take the force of one woman's iron will to stop it in its tracks.

Turns out, Rosa Parks was that woman.

December 1, 1955, started out like any other Thursday for Rosa. She went to her job at the Montgomery Fair department store, where she then worked as a seamstress. When the workday ended, Rosa gathered her purse and coat and walked to the Court Square bus stop. She waited patiently for the Cleveland Avenue bus—the bus she'd taken to and from work many times. When she stepped onto the bus and paid her dime to ride, she immediately spotted an empty seat on the aisle, one row behind the whites-only section of the bus. It was rush hour. Any seat on any bus at this time of day was a blessing. Rosa sat back and gave a quiet sigh of relief.

When the bus stopped to pick up passengers at the Empire Theater stop, six white people got on. They each paid the ten-cent fare, just as

Rosa had done. All but one of them easily found seats at the front of the bus. The sixth passenger, a man, didn't mind standing. He curled his fingers around a holding pole and waited for the bus to pull away.

But according to the bus segregation laws for the state of Alabama, black people were required to give up a bus seat if a white person was left standing. And each bus driver in the state was allowed to lay down the letter of the law on his bus.

As it turned out, Rosa was sitting on the bus that was driven by the same driver who, twelve years before, had kicked Rosa off his bus because she would not enter through the back door. The driver remembered Rosa. And Rosa sure remembered him. He glared at Rosa through his rearview mirror. He ordered her up and out of her seat. But she wouldn't move. Instead, she answered him with a question. Why, she asked, should she have to endure his bossing her around?

Well, the driver didn't take kindly to Rosa challenging him. Next thing Rosa knew, he was standing over her, insisting that she give up her seat to the white man who needed a seat. Rosa clenched her purse, which rested in her lap. When the driver asked Rosa to move a second time, Rosa put it to him plainly and firmly: No.

He told Rosa he would call the police if she didn't move. Rosa didn't flinch. Maybe she was thinking about her grandpa Sylvester's solid belief in not allowing mistreatment from others. Or maybe she was just fed up with giving in to segregation's iron fist. Even the threat of police couldn't rouse Rosa. Once again her answer to the bus driver was simple: Do it. And he did—lickety-split. The police came right away. They arrested Rosa and took her to the city jail. Rosa called her husband and told him the whole story. News of Rosa's arrest had already begun to spread through

Montgomery's black community. Several friends of Rosa's and Raymond's had seen Rosa get arrested. E. D. Nixon from the NAACP was one of the first to hear about Rosa. He immediately collected enough bail money to release Rosa from jail. He told Rosa and Raymond that though the incident was an unfortunate one, it had the power to pound out segregation. If Rosa was willing—and brave enough—to bring a case against Alabama's segregation laws, she could help end segregation in the state.

Rosa didn't have to think long about E. D. Nixon's proposal. Just a short time earlier, Rosa had been staring segregation in the face and saying *no*. Now she was looking the law in the eyes, and without blinking, she said *yes*. She agreed to attack the system that kept her and every black person in the United States of America from being treated equally. Years later, in reflecting on the events that led to her decision, Rosa said, "People always say that I [didn't give] up my seat because I was tired, but that isn't true. I was not tired physically…The only tired I was, was tired of giving in."

On December 5, 1955, Rosa and her attorney, Fred Gray, appeared before Judge John B. Scott in the city court of Montgomery, Alabama. Rosa was found guilty of breaking the Alabama State segregated bus law. She was fined ten dollars. Although Rosa was convicted, her act had ignited the Montgomery bus boycott, a civil rights movement that would change the face of segregation forever.

The Reverend Martin Luther King Jr. helped the boycott get off to a strong start. On the evening of December 5, 1955, he addressed nearly one thousand people at the Holt Street Baptist Church in Montgomery. He said, "We're going to work with grim and firm determination to gain justice on the buses in this city. And...we are not wrong in what we are doing. If we are wrong, the Constitution of the United States is wrong...If we are wrong, justice is a lie. And we are determined here in Montgomery to work and fight until justice runs down like water and righteousness like a mighty stream..."

Martin Luther King's words resonated like thunder on a dark night. The kind of thunder that stirs you from the inside out. As a protest to the treatment they and Rosa had received, every black resident of Montgomery stopped riding the city's buses. They walked to where they wanted to go. They walked miles and miles—to work, to church, to the bank, to the grocery store. They organized car pools. And by denying money to the city bus system, they showed white people that black men and women were valuable paying customers. No matter how tired of walking they may have been—some had to wake up long before dawn to get to work on time—they refused to give up.

Rosa lost her job as a result of her arrest and the boycott. To earn money, she tailored clothes in her home. She spent the rest of her time helping the boycott stay organized. The boycott rolled on for more than a year. Finally, on December 20, 1956, the Supreme Court ruled that in the state of Alabama segregated buses were illegal. Black people went back to riding buses the very next day, and you can best believe that on buses in Montgomery—and throughout the state—black people sat in the front, enjoying their view of justice.

The Montgomery bus boycott was an important triumph for African Americans. It was the beginning of the end of *all* segregation. But it was a victory that came at a cost to Rosa. Soon after the boycott ended, Rosa received angry threats from white people who were in favor of segregation.

A few months later Rosa and Raymond Parks, and Rosa's mother, Leona, moved to Detroit, Michigan, where Rosa's brother had settled.

Living in the North enabled Rosa to continue her civil rights interests peacefully. In 1965 she began working in the office of John Conyers, a young black congressman. As she had done at the NAACP, Rosa kept the congressman's office running smoothly. She also helped him find housing for the city's homeless.

Whenever Rosa saw an opportunity to serve fellow African Americans, she took it. In 1987 she and her husband founded the Rosa and Raymond Parks Institute for Self-Development, a means for teaching young people about civil rights.

Over time Rosa has gained many impressive titles. She has been called the Mother of the Civil Rights Movement and the Patron Saint of the Civil Rights Movement. She even has two streets named after her, one in Detroit, the other in Montgomery. Montgomery's Cleveland Avenue, where Rosa caught the bus on that landmark day in 1955, was later renamed Rosa Parks Boulevard.

No single pronouncement can ever fully capture the impact that Rosa Parks has had on the condition of civil rights in America—and beyond.

Fannie Lou Hamer

Born: Montgomery County, Mississippi • October 6, 1917
Died: Mound Bayou, Mississippi • March 15, 1977

"I question America."

Fannie lou townsend was the youngest of twenty children born to Jim and Lou Ella Townsend. She and her family lived in Sunflower County, Mississippi, in a tumbledown shack that sat on the land of E. W. Brandon, boss man of the Brandon plantation.

The Townsends were sharecroppers by trade. They made their living picking, chopping, and hauling E. W.'s cotton, giving half of all they harvested to E. W. The more cotton they grew, the more they had for themselves. Still, the Townsend family didn't own the land they worked on. They were paid measly wages, and if they had a bad cropping year, they were indebted to E. W. for harvesting supplies. Like many sharecroppers, the Townsends had to work from dawn's first crack till dusk waved a final good-bye. Yet they barely made ends meet.

All the Townsend children picked E. W.'s cotton as soon as they were old enough. The whole family worked that land *hard*, every single day but Sunday, when they worshiped at the Stranger's Home Baptist Church. Stranger's Home taught Fannie Lou the ways of faith. And it was in church that she learned the words to a Negro spiritual that would become her favorite hymn, the hymn people would later associate with her:

This little light of mine
I'm gonna let it shine....
Everywhere I go, I'm gonna let it shine.

When it came time for Fannie Lou to work in E. W.'s cotton fields, she was ready for the challenge. She took to those fields with true enthusiasm. She was more than just a hard worker; she was downright *enterprising*. Fannie Lou was six years old when she went to work in the cotton fields. On her very first day, E. W. told her that if she picked thirty pounds of cotton, he would reward her with cookies and Cracker Jacks.

Since the Townsends didn't have money to buy such goodies, E. W.'s offer was a sweet one to Fannie Lou. She picked the thirty pounds of cotton. The very next week, she picked sixty pounds. And by the time she was thirteen years old, Fannie Lou could snatch up to three hundred pounds of what some folks called the "boll weevil's breakfast."

With the help of Fannie Lou's pickings, the Townsends soon earned enough money to rent their own plot of land. They purchased a small, sturdy house, along with some cows, mules, and chickens. They were free of E. W., and they no longer had to share their crops with anyone but one another.

But not long after they achieved a bit of success, hardship fell upon them. A white man, a neighbor who was jealous of the Townsends' good fortune, poisoned their mules and cows. Without the means to farm, they were forced to move back to the Brandon plantation, back to share-cropping. During the winter, when cotton was scarce, the Townsends had to go "scrapping" for cotton: walking from plantation to plantation, picking cotton leftovers off the frozen ground.

To help provide food for her children, Lou Ella, Fannie's mother, helped slaughter the hogs of plantation owners who lived nearby. The plantation owners paid Lou Ella with pigs' feet and hogs' intestines. Lou Ella cooked up these scraps to make stews and chitterlings for her family.

Then, in 1939, more hardship struck. Fannie Lou's father suffered a stroke and her mother had to provide for the Townsend family on her own. It was the example of Lou Ella's strength and Fannie Lou's own faith that encouraged Fannie Lou to keep on, even when the road got rough.

By the time Fannie Lou was a young woman, she'd had enough of the degrading living conditions that so many black people in the South endured. She wanted to bring about a change to the racial injustices her family and other black people faced. Fannie Lou said, "I asked God to give me a chance to just let me do something about what was going on in Mississippi."

Fannie Lou would get her chance, in more ways than one. In 1944 she married Perry Hamer, a sharecropper who lived on the W. D. Marlowe plantation in Ruleville, a town not far from where Fannie Lou grew up. Everyone called Fannie's husband Pap. Like Fannie Lou's father, Pap was a kindhearted, hardworking man, who supported Fannie Lou's desire to improve the lives of black people.

Fannie Lou and Pap lived and worked on the Marlowe plantation for eighteen years, much the same way Fannie Lou had as a child. She and

Pap worked endless hours in the fields picking, chopping, and hauling cotton. To earn extra money, Fannie Lou scrubbed W. D.'s floors, kept his books, and tended to his children. She even fed his dog and cleaned the bathroom where the dog bathed. It was backbreaking, sweat-raising labor that left little time for much else.

Black people had little say about how unfair the sharecropping system was. But the one thing Fannie Lou often said was, "I'm sick and tired of being sick and tired." This was the motivation that pushed Fannie Lou to fight for the change she'd prayed to God to help her make.

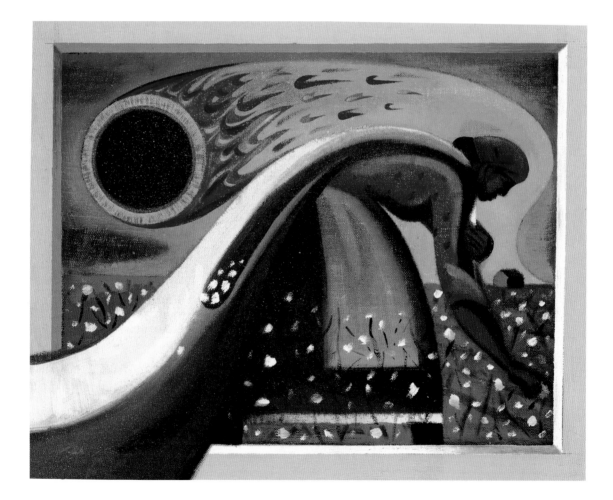

In August 1962, Charles McLaurin, a member of the Student Non-violent Coordinating Committee (SNCC), came to Ruleville to encourage black people to register to vote at the courthouse in Indianola, a town twenty-six miles away. He told local black residents about a mass rally that would explain how voting was the first step in improving conditions for black people in Mississippi. The rally was to be cosponsored by SNCC and the Southern Christian Leadership Conference (SCLC).

Fannie Lou and Pap attended the rally. James Bevel, a field secretary for the SCLC, gave a sermon that stirred up something in Fannie Lou. He talked about a chapter in the Bible, Matthew 16:3, which teaches the importance of paying attention to the happenings in one's community.

Another speaker, James Forman, executive secretary of SNCC, told his listeners that it was their constitutional right to register to vote. Until that night, Fannie Lou and Pap didn't know a black person *could* register to vote. When the leaders of the rally asked anyone willing to go the courthouse and register to vote, to raise their hands, Fannie Lou held her hand up as far as it would go. She was one of the first to volunteer.

Lots of folks kept their hands in their laps, fearing that the white plantation owners they worked for would fire them if they tried to vote. When Fannie Lou later recalled that night, she said, "What was the point of being scared? The only thing they could do to me was kill me, and it seemed like they'd been trying to do that a little bit at a time ever since I could remember."

There were eighteen brave volunteers in all. The following week, on August 31, 1962, they took a bus to Indianola, the county seat, to register. When they arrived at the registrar's office, they were told that in order to vote they would have to take a literacy test. To pass the test, they each had to read aloud for the registrar, who would then decide whether he felt they were qualified to vote or not. Many of Fannie's neighbors didn't know how to read or write. Fannie had had a little schooling and could read and write her own name.

The registrar brought Fannie a hefty black book. He asked her to read and explain the sixteenth section of the Constitution of Mississippi. It was a complicated paragraph about laws—facts that some lawyers didn't even know, let alone sharecroppers! Fannie Lou and all of her friends flunked the test. The experience was humiliating. It left many in the group feeling lower than the curb. To make matters worse, on the way home they were all arrested. The state police claimed that the bus they had taken to get to Indianola was too yellow, that it could be mistaken for a school bus, and that they were breaking the law by riding in it.

Some of the folks seated on that bus were so angry, they saw red. But not Fannie Lou. She stayed cool. She calmed the group of passengers by leading them in a song, "Have a Little Talk with Jesus." For Fannie Lou, making an attempt to vote was the beginning of her work as a civil rights activist.

That evening, back at the Marlowe plantation, W. D. stormed around in a huff. He'd heard about Fannie Lou's trip to Indianola. He ordered her off the plantation by morning, though he insisted that Pap stay on until the harvesting season was over. But Fannie Lou didn't even bother to wait till daybreak. That very night she went to the home of Mrs. Tucker, a friend who lived nearby.

Now the word was out on Fannie Lou. People in Ruleville learned about her bold attempt to vote. And her bravery made lots of folks angry.

Ten days after she'd gone to Mrs. Tucker's, several gunshots were fired into the Tucker house. To this day, it is believed by many people that someone was trying to kill Fannie Lou Hamer because she had taken a stand for her rights.

But Fannie Lou Hamer didn't back down for anybody who tried to stand in her way. She studied the Mississippi State Constitution as if it were the Bible itself. She was determined to pass that test, even if it meant she had to go to Indianola a hundred times. She went to Indianola on two more occasions in an effort to pass the literacy test she needed in order to register to vote. She told the registrar, "I'll be here every thirty days until I pass your test."

On January 10, 1963, one month after Fannie Lou had made her intentions clear to the registrar, she passed the registrar's test. It was her third attempt. She was one of the first black people in Sunflower County, Mississippi, to register to vote. But when voting day came in the fall of 1963, Fannie Lou was turned away at the polls. She was denied her voting privilege because she didn't have enough money to pay the state poll tax.

Gaining the *right* to vote only to have that right snuffed by yet another obstacle spurred Fannie Lou forward. One thing was for certain. Folks could knock Fannie Lou Hamer's persistence, but they couldn't keep her down for long.

Fannie Lou found other ways to fight the complicated voting practices that made it difficult for Southern blacks to vote. She became a member of SNCC and was soon appointed as an SNCC field secretary in Mississippi. As such, Fannie Lou spoke to the people in Ruleville about their voting rights. She organized mass meetings. She preached in churches.

She led the frightened and the weary in song. She even traveled north and encouraged white people to become involved in helping African Americans in the South. And she marched—whether it was pouring rain or hot-as-blazes—in voter-registration demonstrations throughout Mississippi.

It was clear to everyone who knew Fannie Lou Hamer that she was a leader. In June 1963 Fannie Lou attended the annual SNCC conference in Nashville, Tennessee, where she participated in a voter-registration workshop. On the bus trip home, Fannie Lou and several of her friends were arrested, in Winona, Mississippi, for no legal reason at all. They were thrown in jail, where all were brutally beaten—till they bled—by the police. The experience was one Fannie Lou never forgot. It drove her to take the next step in beating back discrimination.

Through her attempts to become a registered voter and her work with the SNCC, Fannie Lou learned that one of the best ways to make the changes she had been praying for was to become active in politics.

In 1964 Fannie Lou and several other SNCC members, including white volunteers who had become active in the cause for civil rights, founded the Mississippi Freedom Democratic Party (MFDP). The purpose of the MFDP was to help African Americans gain greater representation in Mississippi politics. The regular Mississippi Democratic Party, known as the Regulars, did not admit black members at that time. The MFDP included black and white people.

Fannie Lou became the MFDP vice chairperson. Most of her efforts were centered in Mississippi among black people, some of whom were still afraid to speak out for their rights. But Fannie Lou managed to register sixty-three thousand blacks from Mississippi into the party.

In the summer of 1964, Fannie Lou brought the MFDP to national attention. The MFDP chose her and sixty-seven other MFDP delegates to represent them at the Democratic National Convention in Atlantic City, New Jersey. This was where state delegates would select the Democratic candidate for president of the United States. And this was the MFDP's chance to make their presence known to all of America.

But the Democratic Party's Credentials Committee would allow only one group of delegates from Mississippi to be seated as state representatives at the convention. These were the convention rules. The Regulars believed *they* were the official representatives for the state of Mississippi and should be the only ones seated. The MFDP believed they, too, should be seated at the convention. The Credentials Committee would have to choose between the Regulars and the MFDP.

On August 22, 1964, the Credentials Committee gathered to hear the MFDP's side of things. The MFDP had selected Fannie Lou as their spokesperson. Many Americans watched, over a live national television broadcast, as Fannie Lou Hamer—proud, black, and loud—stated her case. She told the American public about the horror, bloodshed, and humiliation African Americans in the South had suffered. She described how it felt to be shut out of the voting polls and excluded from the mainstream political party. She recounted the night she took a beating in Winona. And she told America about her hopes for a better day.

Then she put a charge to the Credentials Committee: "If the Freedom Democratic Party is not seated now, I question America. Is this the America, the land of the free and the home of the brave, where we have to sleep with our telephones off the hook because our lives be threatened daily, because we want to live as decent human beings in America?"

Fannie Lou's presence shone a powerful light on the dark side of discrimination. She was one brave black woman voicing the concerns and aspirations millions of black people carried with them every day. Before Fannie Lou was halfway through, the telephones at the Credentials Committee headquarters rang and rang with calls from people urging the Committee to allow the MFDP delegation to be seated at the convention.

In response the Committee offered a compromise. They would allow the MFDP to be unofficial "at-large" delegates and would let the MFDP seat *two* of their sixty-eight delegates with *all* of the delegates from the Regulars. Fannie Lou objected to the compromise. "We didn't come all this way for no two seats when all of us is tired," she said. But the compromise was set. After two more nights of returning to the convention, trying to get seated, Fannie Lou and the MFDP boarded a bus and went back to Mississippi.

Even though the MFDP was not seated at the 1964 Democratic National Convention, Fannie Lou Hamer's presence there was unforgettable. After the convention, the MFDP's membership grew. Even some of the Regulars were so taken with Fannie Lou's speech, they, too, became members of the MFDP. The party changed its name to the Mississippi Loyalist Democratic Party.

In August 1968 the Democratic National Convention was held in Chicago, Illinois. For a second time the Credentials Committee tried to issue a seating compromise. Again Fannie Lou refused. This time her tenacity paid off: She and the other delegates were seated at the convention.

When Fannie Lou took her seat, everyone on the convention floor rose from their chairs to give her a standing ovation! Fannie Lou Hamer had spent much of her life standing up for the rights of black people. Now it was her turn to have all kinds of people stand up for her.

Shirley Chisholm

Born: Brooklyn, New York • November 20, 1924

"The time has come to change America. Someday, somewhere, somehow, someone other than a white male could be President."

WHEN SHIRLEY ANITA ST. HILL was three years old, her parents, Charles and Ruby, sent her and her younger sisters, Odessa and Muriel, to the West Indian island of Barbados to live on their grandmother's farm. It was hard for Charles to earn a solid living on the meager salary he made as a baker's helper. Shirley's parents wanted to buy a house, and they wanted their daughters to have proper schooling. They didn't *want* to send their daughters away, but they thought letting Grandmother Emily help raise their children was a way to save the money they needed, and a chance to give Shirley and her sisters a good education.

Grandmother Emily's sunny village was a far cry from the streets of Brooklyn, the New York City borough where Shirley was born. The St. Hill girls missed their parents, but they took well to island life, and they were well taken care of. Grandmother Emily insisted that each child do her share of farm chores. She also saw to it that Shirley and her sisters attended church regularly. On Sundays, when it came time to dress in their finest clothes and walk the two miles to worship services, Shirley, Odessa, and Muriel went along willingly with their grandmother. Sundays were special to Shirley because after church their aunt Myrtle and uncle Lincoln and Shirley's cousins and neighbors gathered for supper. Sunday dinners were rich with fruits and vegetables from the island.

When Shirley was four years old, Grandmother Emily enrolled her in school, held in the village church. This school was a traditional British-style school, common in Barbados. The teachers didn't tolerate anyone who wasn't serious about learning. It was not the place for complaining, back talk, or making faces. Seven classes—set apart only by chalkboards—met in the same room. Shirley learned with children of all ages. Even as a little girl, she was a good student. She could read and write clearly by the time she was five years old.

Back in Brooklyn, Shirley's parents were blessed with another daughter, Selma. But they had suffered financial hardship during the Great Depression, and after the birth of their fourth child they realized they could not afford to buy a house. Seven years had passed since they'd taken Shirley, Odessa, and Muriel to Barbados. They felt it best to bring their family together again.

Shirley was ten years old when she and her sisters returned to Brooklyn. She was glad to be reunited with her mother and father, and was happy to meet baby Selma for the first time. But there wasn't much else in New York City to put a smile on Shirley's face. After all, New York was crowded—and it was *cold*. And to make matters worse, Shirley had to start school in the third grade.

In Barbados she had been in classes that were equivalent to the sixth grade. But because she had not been taught American history or geography, the teachers at her school, P.S. 84, held her back. School became drudgery for Shirley. She could read and write circles around most kids her age, let alone *third* graders. Thanks to one observant teacher who saw that Shirley was a bright child and suggested she have a private tutor, Shirley caught up in the subjects she hadn't learned.

At home Shirley received a valuable education, too. Though her parents had had little formal schooling, they taught her lessons that would shape her future in ways no classroom could. Shirley's father loved to read. Even on his small salary he always purchased several newspapers each day. It was important to Charles St. Hill that he and his daughters understand world events and the happenings in their own community, especially issues that affected the rights of black people.

Shirley's father was a follower of Marcus Garvey, a civil rights leader from Jamaica. Charles St. Hill impressed upon his children the importance of learning African American history. Both Shirley's parents encouraged her to visit the Brooklyn Public Library to find books about black men and women who had devoted themselves to the struggle for racial justice.

The library became a friend to Shirley. There she took a special interest in how Harriet Tubman had led so many slaves to freedom along the Underground Railroad. Harriet Tubman's accomplishments showed Shirley that women could be leaders—that a single black woman could lead legions of people, even when a mountain of obstacles stood in her way.

In 1942 Shirley graduated from Girls' High School in Brooklyn. Her good grades had put her at the top of her class. Soon after graduation, she enrolled at Brooklyn College, where she learned there was more to education than book learning. For Shirley, college was a lesson in black pride. Shirley had hoped to become a teacher, but college introduced a new idea.

During her second year at Brooklyn College, Shirley joined the Harriet Tubman Society, a civil rights club whose members met regularly to discuss ways to lessen the racial tensions between black people and white people. Shirley had lots of good ideas for helping African Americans gain equality. She spoke up at club meetings and during her classes. And she listened to the views of others, whether they agreed with her side of things or not.

Once, a white politician came to Brooklyn College to speak to the students. In his speech he said, "Black people will advance someday, but black people are always going to need white people leading them." This comment made Shirley very angry. Even before the man was done speaking, Shirley decided that she was not going to accept such stupidity.

Shirley's friends—both black and white—began to point out her talents for encouraging others, organizing groups, speaking in public, and putting her ideas into action. Then one of Shirley's favorite teachers, political science professor Louis Warsoff, a white man who was blind, encouraged Shirley to consider a career in politics. Shirley appreciated Professor Warsoff's suggestion but dismissed it quickly. To her a political career was a far-fetched notion. She told Professor Warsoff, "You forget that I am black—and I'm a woman."

But then Shirley remembered how angry it made her that some people believed African Americans could not lead themselves—and she remembered all she'd learned about Harriet Tubman's courage.

Professor Warsoff helped Shirley set her eyes on the prize of a life in politics. She began to attend meetings of local political groups. She discovered that a political career meant taking the lead in helping others make positive changes in their communities. It meant working to change the laws and government policies that affected housing, schools, health care, and, of course, race relations.

After graduating from Brooklyn College, in 1946, Shirley worked as a teacher at Mount Calvary Child Care Center in Harlem. She enrolled at Columbia University, where she took night courses toward a master's degree in education. The Columbia master's program required hard work and long study hours, but Shirley met the challenge. And she met a smart study companion, a dashing Jamaican man who was also earning a master's degree at Columbia. His name was Conrad Chisholm. He and Shirley became good friends. Conrad had an easygoing way about him, and he was bright and ambitious like Shirley. In 1949 Shirley and Conrad married, and settled in Brooklyn.

Shirley continued her work as a teacher. At the same time, her interest in politics continued to grow. It grew out of what Shirley observed every time she attended a meeting of the local Democratic Party. She saw that black people were considered second-class citizens by many members of the party—that when an African American presented an idea, it was ousted right away. For black *women* who attended Democratic Party meetings, it was worse. Black women weren't even considered second-class citizens. They weren't considered at all. For Shirley Chisholm—a well-spoken, intelligent woman who was always brimming with good ideas—this was unacceptable.

Rather than continue attending Democratic Party meetings, only to feel belittled and useless, Shirley helped form the Unity Democratic Club, a group of black men and women who, like Shirley, had an interest in politics.

As much as Shirley enjoyed sharing her political views with other African Americans, she discovered that sexism was just as prevalent among black men as it was among white men. In 1964 when Shirley decided to run for office in the New York State Assembly, the Unity Club men told her that as a woman, she could certainly take part in club activities, but running for public office was best left to men.

Well, these foolish attitudes didn't stop Shirley. They had the opposite effect. She launched her own campaign and won the election. As New York's second assemblywoman (a woman named Bessie Buchanan was the first), Shirley wasted not one minute of her time putting her appointment into action. She introduced several important bills that became laws, including one that increased unemployment benefits for domestic workers, such as housekeepers and cooks.

People began to see that Shirley Chisholm was serious about making a difference. She was elected to the state assembly for a second term, and created a bill to help start a program called SEEK, which gave college scholarships to black high school students.

Shirley was on a steady climb. Her success in the state assembly encouraged her to run for Congress, in 1968. She ran for a seat in the Twelfth Congressional District of Brooklyn, a new district that included the community of Bedford-Stuyvesant, the neighborhood where Shirley grew up.

But in her race for Congress, Shirley faced a tough opponent, a Republican candidate named James Farmer, one of the founders of the Congress for Racial Equality (CORE). James Farmer was a well-known civil rights activist who was as outspoken as Shirley. During the campaign, he publicly questioned Shirley's abilities. He told voters that a man, not a women, could best represent Brooklyn's Twelfth District in Congress.

Shirley let James brag all he wanted. His platform helped her build a strong campaign based on her greatest strength—being a woman. After all, who primarily organized the day-to-day duties of a household? *Women.* Who managed most school classrooms? *Women.* Who were experts in child care? *Women.* And it was *women* who voted Shirley Chisholm into Congress—allowing her to beat out James Farmer two-to-one—and elected Shirley as the first black woman to serve in the House of Representatives.

As a congresswoman, Shirley worked hard on behalf of her district. She helped people in Bedford-Stuyvesant find jobs. She fought discrimination and spoke out for the rights of poor people and children. And she showed her Brooklyn neighbors how to navigate the web of government agencies that set policies for housing, education, and health services. When Shirley's first term in Congress ended, she ran for re-election and won. She would serve in Congress for a total of seven terms, from 1968 to 1982.

In 1970, as the 1972 presidential election approached, Shirley's friends and supporters urged her to run for president of the United States. Shirley shrugged off her friends' suggestion. How could *she* run for president? She had achieved success in Congress, but running for president was a different story. Presidential candidates need money to run their campaigns. They need a staff of devoted workers to keep their campaigns going. And they need *votes.*

But more and more, people kept pressing Shirley to run. And soon their desire to see Shirley go for it rubbed off. She decided to enter the race and to give it all she had. She was the first African American woman ever to seek a presidential nomination from a major political party.

In order to run for president, Shirley first needed to win enough votes to become elected as the Democratic Party presidential candidate. Then if elected to represent the Democratic Party, she would run against the Republican presidential candidate. In 1972 Richard Nixon, a Republican, was the president of the United States, and he intended to run for re-

election. Several Democrats, all white men, sought the Democratic Party nomination. There were senators Hubert Humphrey from Minnesota, George McGovern from South Dakota, and Edmund Muskie from Maine.

Shirley knew she was an underdog in the race. But that didn't matter to her. What was most important was that she stuck to her belief that she had just as much to offer the American people as any of the other candidates. Shirley traveled from state to state to spread her message. She told people, "The time has come to change America. Someday, somewhere, somehow, someone other than a white male could be President."

On January 25, 1972, Shirley Chisholm officially announced her candidacy. She said: "I am not the candidate of black America, although I am black and proud. I am not the candidate for the women's movement of this country, although I am a woman...I am the candidate of the people."

Although Shirley won the support of many, she lost the Democratic nomination to Senator George McGovern. But Shirley didn't see her loss as a defeat. The fact that she had entered the race was a victory to her. Because of Shirley, many black people registered to vote for the first time in their lives. Many women, who had always left politics to men, took active roles in the political process. When the election was over, Shirley told newspaper reporters that her campaign opened doors to future candidates who may not have run otherwise.

It wasn't long before others took Shirley's lead. In 1984 Geraldine Ferraro, a white congresswoman from Queens, New York, ran for vice president of the United States. Jesse Jackson, a black Baptist minister from Greenville, South Carolina, ran for president twice, once in 1984 and again in 1988. Shirley's example paved the way for Geraldine and Jesse. And it proved to everyone else that a little girl from Brooklyn, whose parents could not afford to buy a home, could dare to dream of becoming the number-one tenant of the White House. Shirley had been right: America was changing.

For Further Reading

1. GENERAL HISTORICAL COLLECTIONS

Bogin, Ruth, and Bert James Loewenberg, eds. *Black Women in Nineteenth-Century American Life: Their Words, Their Thoughts, Their Feelings.* University Park, Pa.: Pennsylvania State Univ. Press, 1976.

Boyd, Herb. *Down the Glory Road.* New York: Avon Books, 1995.

Carson, Clayborne, David J. Garrow, Gerald Gill, Vincent Harding, Darlene Clark Hine, eds. *The Eyes on the Prize: Civil Rights Reader: Documents, Speeches, and Firsthand Accounts from the Black Freedom Struggle, 1954–1990.* New York: Viking Penguin, 1991.

Fireside, Bryna J. *Is There a Woman in the House…or Senate?* Morton Grove, Ill.: Albert Whitman & Co., 1994.

Frazier, Thomas R., ed. *Afro-American History: Primary Sources.* New York: Harcourt Brace Jovanovich, 1970.

Haskins, James. *Get on Board: The Story of the Underground Railroad.* New York: Scholastic, 1993.

———. *One More River to Cross: The Stories of Twelve Black Americans.* New York: Scholastic, 1992.

Hine, Darlene Clark, ed. *Black Women in America: An Historical Encyclopedia.* Vol. 2, *M–Z.* Brooklyn: Carlson Publishing, 1993.

Igus, Toyomi, ed. *Great Women in the Struggle.* Orange, N.J.: Just Us Books, 1991.

Katz, William Loren. *Black Legacy: A History of New York's African Americans.* New York: Atheneum Books for Young Readers, 1997.

——. *Black Women of the Old West.* New York: Atheneum Books for Young Readers, 1995.

Kazickas, Jurate, and Lynn Sherr. *Susan B. Anthony Slept Here: A Guide to American Women's Landmarks.* New York: Times Books, 1994.

Lanker, Brian. *I Dream a World: Portraits of Black Women Who Changed America.* New York: Stewart, Tabori & Chang, 1989; distributed in U.S. by Workman Publishing.

Litwack, Leon, and August Meier, eds. *Black Leaders of the Nineteenth Century.* Champaign, Ill.: Univ. of Illinois, 1988.

Schlissel, Lillian. *Black Frontiers: A History of African American Heroes in the Old West.* New York: Simon & Schuster Books for Young Readers, 1995.

Smith, Jessie Carney, ed. *Notable Black American Women.* Detroit: Gale Research, 1992.

Taylor, Kimberly Hayes. *Black Civil Rights Champions.* Minneapolis: Oliver Press, 1995.

2. BIOGRAPHIES OF THE FREEDOM FIGHTERS

Krass, Peter. *Sojourner Truth.* Black Americans of Achievement Series. New York: Chelsea House Publishers, 1988.

McKissack, Patricia C., and Frederick McKissack. *Sojourner Truth–Ain't I a Woman?* New York: Scholastic, 1992.

Elish, Dan. *Harriet Tubman and the Underground Railroad.* Brookfield, Conn.: Millbrook Press, 1993.

Klots, Steve. *Ida Wells-Barnett.* Black Americans of Achievement Series. New York: Chelsea House Publishers, 1994.

Medearis, Angela Shelf. *Princess of the Press: The Story of Ida B. Wells-Barnett.* New York: Lodestar Books, 1997.

Greenfield, Eloise. *Mary McLeod Bethune.* New York: Thomas Y. Crowell Co., 1977.

Halasa, Malu. *Mary McLeod Bethune.* Black Americans of Achievement Series. New York: Chelsea House Publishers, 1993.

Dallard, Shyrlee. *Ella Baker: A Leader Behind the Scenes.* Englewood Cliffs, N.J.: Silver Burdett Press, 1990.

Friese, Kai Jabir. *Rosa Parks: The Movement Organizes.* Englewood Cliffs, N.J.: Silver Burdett Press, 1990.

Hull, Mary. *Rosa Parks.* Black Americans of Achievement Series. New York: Chelsea House Publishers, 1994.

Parks, Rosa. *Dear Mrs. Parks: A Dialogue with Today's Youth.* New York: Lee & Low Books, 1996.

Parks, Rosa, and Jim Haskins. *Rosa Parks: My Story.* New York: Dial Books, 1992.

Colman, Penny. *Fannie Lou Hamer and the Fight for the Vote.* Brookfield, Conn.: Millbrook Press, 1993.

Jordan, June. *Fannie Lou Hamer.* New York: Thomas Y. Crowell Co., 1972.

Mills, Kay. *This Little Light of Mine: The Life of Fannie Lou Hamer.* New York: Dutton, 1993.

Rubel, David. *Fannie Lou Hamer: From Sharecropping to Politics.* Englewood Cliffs, N.J.: Silver Burdett Press, 1990.

Chisholm, Shirley. *The Good Fight.* New York: Harper & Row, 1973.

——. *Unbought and Unbossed.* Boston: Houghton Mifflin, 1970.

Scheader, Catherine. *Shirley Chisholm: Teacher and Congresswoman.* Hillsdale, N.J.: Enslow Publishers, 1990.